ALSO BY CARLY SIMON

Boys in the Trees: A Memoir

Touched by the Sun

Touched
by the Sun

My Friendship with Jackie

CARLY SIMON

FARRAR, STRAUS AND GIROUX   *New York*

Farrar, Straus and Giroux
120 Broadway, New York 10271

Printed in the United States of America
First edition, 2019

Grateful acknowledgment is made for permission to reprint lines from
"You Have Called Me by Name," by Joseph Tetlow, S.J., from *Hearts
on Fire: Praying with Jesuits,* edited by Michael Harter, S.J. (Chestnut
Hill, MA: Institute of Jesuit Sources, 1993), page 14.

Library of Congress Cataloging-in-Publication Data
Names: Simon, Carly, author.
Title: Touched by the sun : my friendship with Jackie / Carly Simon.
Description: First edition. | New York : Farrar, Straus and Giroux,
    2019.
Identifiers: LCCN 2019020329 | ISBN 9780374277727 (hardcover)
Subjects: LCSH: Simon, Carly—Friends and associates. | Onassis,
    Jacqueline Kennedy, 1929–1994. | Singers—United States—
    Biography. | Presidents' spouses—United States—Biography.
Classification: LCC ML420.S56296 A3 2019 | DDC 782.42164092
    [B]—dc23
LC record available at https://lccn.loc.gov/2019020329

Designed by Richard Oriolo

Our books may be purchased in bulk for promotional, educational, or
business use. Please contact your local bookseller or the Macmillan
Corporate and Premium Sales Department at 1-800-221-7945, extension
5442, or by e-mail at MacmillanSpecialMarkets@macmillan.com.

www.fsgbooks.com
www.twitter.com/fsgbooks • www.facebook.com/fsgbooks

10   9   8   7   6   5   4   3   2   1

To all my first girlfriends, the ones I knew from a very young age, who made the greatest impact on my life and who remain very much an integral part of it

Ellen, Jennie Lou, Jesse, Nan, Tamara

One must still have chaos in oneself to be able to give birth to a dancing star.

—FRIEDRICH NIETZSCHE
 (TRANSLATED BY WALTER KAUFMANN)

Contents

Touched by the Sun

Prologue

YOU CAN'T RECAPTURE people who are gone—not exactly, not entirely. You can imagine their faces, or their bodies, or their hands, but those images are like stills, or paintings in frames. The other times, when they crossed their arms, made sudden or tender gestures, flattened down the crease in their trousers, lowered their gaze, smoothed away a bang—those images of movement, of animation—are gone. I don't know where. The past.

You can recall the silver in their voice, or that unusual word choice, or the extending of an emphasis like a damper pedal pressed on a syllable. It's harder to remember their voice when they asked a waiter for some lemon, or complimented your blouse, or noticed how late it was getting. Recapturing fluid images of people as they were in life, while they keep morphing and resisting you, is nearly impossible. But you *can* remember how they made you feel.

How, then, do you shape a somewhat reliable portrait of someone, anyone? Pin them down? Sweep up all the parts to gather and form a whole with all the details intact? You can't. There just aren't enough words to pick out all those in-between moments: the voyage of someone's eyes when the conversation she's having falters; her expression as she's deciding between the veal cutlet or the veal tortellini; the movement in her brow, a possible giveaway. Most languages have words that don't and can't translate, that have more refined, nuanced meanings, like the fifty-something Eskimo versions of the word "snow." In-between moments are like that.

Writing about someone is like describing the changing sky. Catch those cirrus clouds as they form a chiffon scarf, before turning into a swan and, a few seconds later, a swarm of pale eels swimming in a cold blue stream. Some wintry skies have snow flurries like those in a movie I loved, while others I can liken to an afternoon wind lifting my grandmother's cheeks with gusty intention. Trying to bring accuracy to a written account of a person is this hard. Almost all you can hope to accomplish is to capture the essence of who they were to you—what your experience of them was.

How do you write about a close friend? And what if that close friend was a well-known someone like Jacqueline Kennedy Onassis? She, who was such a prominent person that she will be remembered forever, whatever *forever* turns out to be. Each time I saw her anew, I realized again this was Jackie. No matter how she succeeded in making me feel an equal, she was still *Jackie*. I tried to overcome this feeling, but could never really shed it. It had grown up around me as a child and seeped into my unconscious that her aura was not, and never would be, like anyone else's.

I'm not sure I'll ever think of her as in the past. And my knowing Jackie in the way that I did is almost embarrassing because in my description of her, I will never be able to do her justice. Did I know enough of those wonderful little details that round out a person? Did she ever study a *Michelin Guide*, or glance down at a map while she was driving? In how many languages had she learned to say, "I hope you liked my husband's speech—we are so appreciative of your hospitality"? And in how many languages did she know how to say a polite version of "Get me the hell out of here"?

Any effort to put together some memories risks ridicule or denouncement. *What does* she *know? Why* did *Jackie spend so much time with her?* There might also be resentment.

And resentment is a tricky business. Some people may just not like it that I knew Jackie. Or that I may have known a different Jackie than her other friends. Did she reveal more of herself to them? Did she tell someone else that she liked French mustard, or that she preferred the imported Italian kind with horseradish? Did she talk about love?

In Jackie's descriptions to me of a trip she'd taken, what percentage of my recollections include a memory so subjective that its intended meaning, through the passing of time, has been lost? Except maybe a reveal in her facial expression, or an inadvertent tic of her wrist—gestures I might possibly have attached to another conversation on another day that she and I would have one or two or five years later.

Other questions I wonder about, little things I would have loved the answers to: About how many people that Jackie or I mentioned in a conversation did she have memories or knowledge of that she kept to herself? How did she feel when she was about to jump her horse over a high fence? Did she prefer the mezzo-soprano voice to that of the coloratura? Did she ever look in the mirror and worry she was going to have to pay attention to yet another slope, once a sweet dimple, now possibly a crease? How many minutes a day did she spend putting on creams and lotions? Did the moon affect her spirits? Did she believe it did?

As much time as Jackie and I spent together in the ten years I knew her, I forgot to ask her what her favorite flower was. Or maybe I did, but have forgotten the answer, though

I could always look it up. But the answer I find might be wrong, or the flower her favorite only if it was a velvety light coral. With someone that well-known, your brain cannot help but sift through other people's images and words. When I met Jackie, many of our interactions were influenced by the media—newsreels, newspaper articles, books—history. Over time, the Jackie I knew came to bear only a partial resemblance to the impression I'd had before.

The best I can do is to tell you what I remember. To show *enough* of her. To write down the parts that left a lasting impression. Some interchange, some anecdote recorded in my diary soon enough after it happened that I could separate it from the chorus of crickets that fill my head when I think about her. I can tell you some things about Jackie that changed me. That comforted me. That made me laugh or cry. I can tell you about the moments in our relationship that reminded me so much of my relationship with my mother that in time I began to see Jackie, and our friendship, through a new lens. But in the end, my portrait will still be only a fraction, a trace, a quarter tone, another ounce of blue added to the rose quartz. A painter's palette gone off its rocker from trying too hard.

How do you make the sky truly moonlit?

Of course New York in those days

Was carriage rides and matinees

He took her to a ball

At the Waldorf Astoria

He would fall for her

Fall for her, he would fall

—"HELLO BIG MAN"

1

Carriage Rides and Matinees

B Y THE LATE 1980S, the Upper West Side of Manhattan had lost some crucial part of its innocence.
The remainders of its old-world heritage had grown
to accommodate a newer kind of tenant. That isn't to say its
charm was lost—not completely. But in the past decade,
many of the things I'd loved most about the once run-down
blocks just west of Central Park—antique stores, barber-
shops, family-owned delicatessens—had been replaced
by less bohemian, tonier—mind you, quite lovely—richer

people's gathering spots: the Mexican restaurant Santa Fe, Café Columbus, Café Luxembourg, Café La Fortuna . . . and Café des Artistes, where I was headed one slushy, wind-pummeled early afternoon in March.

During the 1970s and most of the 1980s, the apartments along the western stretch of Central Park in the Sixties and Seventies were comfy and unconventional, crammed with bookshelves and proudly shabby furniture. But gone were the days when artists could survive in rent-controlled spaces, immigrants ran mom-and-pop businesses, and psychiatrists nodded behind double-thick doors in roomy suites whirring with white noise. Some tenants held on to their rent-protected apartments, and couples could still be glimpsed on fire escapes drinking wine out of paper cups at dusk. But in general, the gentrification of the Upper West Side north of Lincoln Center had come on pretty fast.

Almost overnight, doormen with spiffier sartorial upgrades appeared, opening the just-cleaned-and-polished brass doors of impressive prewar buildings like the Dakota, the Kenilworth, and the San Remo that looked out over Central Park. At the start of the twentieth century, these lonely outposts stood at the desolate edge of the Park. But by the early 1980s, their co-ops and rentals were fresh on the market and in demand. Rambling, tall-ceilinged suites of rooms were being snatched up like *Billboard* ads by show business and music mogul folks. Other than parts of upper-crust Fifth Avenue, these majestic Beaux Arts–style buildings became some of the most desirable residences in New York. I lived in one of them: the Langham, between Seventy-third and Seventy-fourth Streets.

It was March 21, the first day of spring, but you would have never guessed it. I'd read recently that the ancient calendars pointed to March 21 as a magical day, one blessed with hours in equal proportion—twelve and twelve— of light and dark. Did a certain balance prevail? I wasn't feeling it. From Seventy-third Street, I began making my way south. The wind coming in off the Hudson River, five blocks to the west, was slashing, and with each gust I was forced to alter the position and the angle of my now nearly pointless scarf. Again and again the fabric of my clothing became untethered from my body, exposing triangles of my neck and chest to the buffeting will of the wind. Then came the snowflakes, fat, freakish, and out of nowhere. As I struggled pointlessly to keep myself covered, I wondered why, like me, no one around me was dressed for the weather. But back then, we didn't know everything the way we do now. Weather reports were still excitingly unreliable.

It was 1:25 p.m.; I was already nearly half an hour late for my lunch date. I bumped into people who held their umbrellas down low to fend off the western winds at cross streets, releasing them only when tall buildings could shield them from the wildest gusts. Soon the snow turned to sleet. Snubbing our umbrellas and hats, the needles of ice hammered our heads as we prepped for the next cross street and the next whippingly windy onslaught. Closing in on one intersection after another, we were a synchronized swarm, tightening our collars and scarves around our necks and faces like sailors reefing their sails against an approaching squall. It isn't the wind but the setting of sails that keeps you out of harm's way.

In the end, I decided to run the remaining distance to the corner of Sixty-seventh Street and Central Park West, and from there to Café des Artistes, which was in the middle of the block. It was the most French of all the cafés, and the one where today I was having lunch with the Bouvier in my life, Jacqueline Kennedy Onassis.

AS I APPROACHED the entrance, I saw that Café des Artistes' definitively lush holiday window boxes were still in place, clustered with Christmas greens and fairy-garden white lights. Considering it was the first day of spring, I understood that this sparkly gesture belonged somewhere in the category of "keeping love alive." Hold on to the spirit of Christmas until you stumble into a tulip on Park Avenue.

I was late, very late, and the only thing left was for me to come up with a little white lie. Was that permissible? What would be my excuse, or excuses? Jackie was never late. By then I had known her, better and better, for two years, and never once during that time had she ever shown up even a few minutes after she said she would—not at a dinner at my house in Martha's Vineyard, not at my apartment in New York, not for a publisher's meeting, not for a scheduled phone call, not for a shopping trip, not even for the movies we went to on so many Thursday afternoons when she took off a half day.

As the wind blasted me through the swinging doors and into the lobby of the des Artistes building, I remembered advice attributed to W. C. Fields: *if you can't dazzle them with brilliance, baffle them with bullshit*. Could I even manage to baffle with bullshit? What would my little white lie be? I felt so awful. Oh, Jackie, how could I leave you waiting for more than half an hour? It was unacceptable. Even knowing her as well as I did, she was, for me, still at that juncture more a black-and-white photo than a confidante and close friend—not someone with whom I could be casually tardy.

But she hadn't arrived yet. Had I gotten the hour wrong? The day? The week?

Inside the restaurant, the concierge, headwaiter, and coat girl greeted me simultaneously, asking in melodic, crisscrossing French if they could bring a glass of wine, some hot tea—a cup of cocoa, perhaps—to my table while I waited for Ms. Onassis to arrive? They must have sensed how much I enjoyed the attention, but from years of being on both sides of that experience, I knew enough to see through any shows of Uriah Heep–like deference. Hadn't my own mother taught me the words "sycophant" and "obsequious"?

"Ms. Onassis generally likes this back table"—the head-waiter led me to a corner of the restaurant—"and you can get a nice view of the snow and also be out of the draft." I sat down, and a moment later a basket of breads arrived—sourdough rolls mixed with breadsticks, mostly, a delicious combination of sweet and savory, hard and soft. I took a sip of my wine, which had come to the table heated, with a cinnamon stick as a stirrer. "*Détendez vous, Madame*," murmured at least two of the waiters, one after the next, as they swiveled through the crowded room. Just maybe, they imagined, I would praise their service to Ms. Onassis. Certainly I saw no other cinnamon sticks in any other glasses of wine.

Café des Artistes was my favorite place to eat whenever I was fulfilling a desire for something expensive and slightly formal. As usual, I became transfixed by the murals covering nearly every wall, the same ones I'd admired through so many years of dining there—those dependable, beautiful girls, hazily elastic on their swings. The mural girls might just as easily have been glimpsed along the pathways and lawns of Sarah Lawrence, which I attended for two years in the 1960s. I was not jealous of those mural girls. I knew they posed no immediate threat. I couldn't be appreciably jealous of a painting of a woman, however translucent or curvaceous she might be. Nor did I wonder if these rosy girls went to college. I had, but I still couldn't figure out when to bring the zero down and move the decimal point to the left.

The mural girls were all so blissful; their navels—a feature always favored by their painters—looked like pale green kiwis just bitten into. Up close, you could peer way down deep into their mysteriousness. The more imaginative could go for a drifting, lapping paddle alongside these cherubic lasses and hear a new kind of song. No chirping birds, just lengthy, sustained watery sounds or, better yet, melodies that rode the surface of the rocks, every note soaked, pushing and pulling against the chord of the water.

Compared to the murals' sun-sprayed and -streaked, orchid-y lavender, the tablecloths in the room seemed like mundane burnt-out fields; the diners caught up in a gauze of yellow, filtering to baby blue suffused with sun—or was it more like butter carried by starlight? I was lost in my rosy-mural-girl fugue, but I stopped short and was reassured that I hadn't actually said that out loud—that bit about the butter! (Maybe something for a song later.)

IT WAS TEN MINUTES before two, and I was starting to get alarmed. It had gone way past the point of *This isn't like Jackie*. Nor were there any whispered messages from the concierge or the waiter, who kept refilling my drink and my bread basket. Every time one of them came back to the table with the diversion of a few pickled herring, or another touch-up of warm wine, I asked them first in words and, after the fourth round, with my eyes and then eyelashes only: *Have you had any word from Ms. Onassis?* Their answers were consistently comforting: "I'm sure with this weather she couldn't find a cab." "Ms. Onassis isn't the kind of lady who demands a limousine to take her around town." "You don't worry, Mrs. . . . ah yes, Msss . . . Mademoiselle."

The final time, as the waiter walked away, my heart began to race. Then, a moment of clarity, and another voice: *I am nothing. I do nothing. I mean nothing. So why don't I just order some really expensive brandy and Jackie (if she ever comes—oh, God, where is Jackie, anyway?) will see it on the bill and frown with disapproval?* I've always felt safer when I was out of earshot of this voice: the observing ego, the judge, the gavel, the authority on my failures, the feeling of un-belonging, the carbonation that is my anxiety. What triggered it in that moment? A memory of being locked in my mother's car when I was five while she, unbeknownst to me, was waiting in line at the bank? Or just the fear that Jackie had changed her mind about me, had stood me up, decided I wasn't worth knowing further? This voice, which plagued me all my life, was coming more frequently these days.

Overly conscious of my heart beating in my chest, I tried

to refocus on the swinging maidens, but in my consterna-
tion, their bas-relief sexy white swan persona wasn't working for me anymore. I signaled to the waiter and ordered two
brandies. After taking a big swallow from one, the room in
all its colors and appliqués began closing in on me. I was the
girl on the swing, I told myself, just the girl on the swing, my
legs pointing off to the east as another girl sent me further
sailing into the damp secret worlds of the mural girls. But I
couldn't quite find myself among them. I was just a watcher,
not *one of*, not *a member of*, or *a part of* as I had recently felt,
but a lone observer of the smiling, posing, perching, pranc-
ing, insouciant, nubile, lovingly painted girls all around me.
I spent the next hour or so perched on one of those swings,
feeling drunk-ish. The brandy had begun to relax me, and I
sat in the garden until it became a part of me.

RETURNING MY CONSCIOUSNESS to the dining room, I
felt a funny, sudden wooziness. I got up from the table, feign-
ing lucidity, and took my own time swanning past the tables
of chic diners appreciating the salmon four ways—a specialty of the house—until I got to the ladies' room.

The mirror above the sink revealed a stunned, pained,
worried, pale face. "Change that expression, darling, it makes
your pretty face so ugly!" my mother used to say to me. My
shame glared back at me, magnified by its exposure in the
mirror. I looked as though I'd been caught naked in church.

I still blamed myself for my panic attacks, as if they were an indication of a weak character, a flaw. An undeveloped will. Should I call Jackie? Try to track her down at the office or her apartment? What if she'd been struck down on the street? Removing my antique pill case from my fancy pocketbook, I furrowed through pellets of all different colors and sizes until I found the one I wanted. Sliding it out, I checked the color (yellow, with a cutout heart in the center, like some grown-up, devilish version of children's candy) before crushing the Valium between my teeth, mixing it into a chalky paste, and swallowing it. *Please, please, Jackie, come.*

Jackie and I were relatively new friends and there was still so much we didn't know about each other—so much adapting still to do to each other's rhythms (would we?). I hadn't told her about the boy who had introduced me to sex in our pool house in Stamford, Connecticut, when I was only eight years old. Or about the very low depths my self-esteem sometimes scraped up against. I hadn't told her much about my ex-husband, James Taylor, or how sad I'd been growing of late, the sadness like some dark bubble around me, strangling all air and circulation. I longed to reveal myself to her. To cut out the fluff, excise the formality. I longed for her to reciprocate, but knew it would be out of line, out of time, out of the question. I wanted to cry, to tell her how sometimes I felt so out of my mind I could barely leave my apartment— and yes, I was prone to exaggerating, but I also *believed* my exaggerations! But telling her what a wreck I could be would be too messy, too intrusive. She probably had some notion already.

For the next ten minutes I sat frozen on the closed toilet seat, waiting for something, not knowing what that something was, responding to one or two knocks from outside with the strained brightness of a parakeet: "Sorry!" and "I'll be out in a sec!" After a minute, I heard another knock on the door. "Just a minute," I said, the parakeet replaced by some sterner bird.

I got up, faced the mirror, and put on some blush and lipstick—enough so that I looked alive, at least—and quickly brushed my stringy, damp hair. When I got back to my table, the seat across from mine was still empty. But there was good news. *Everything is well*, the waiter confided. *Ms. Onassis was in an elevator that got stuck in her office building, but she's fine and will be here in five minutes.*

Somewhere in those pre-cell-phone days, and in the depths of my mind, I must have known Jackie was all right all along. She had been through so many fearsome experiences that getting stuck in an elevator was probably the equivalent of "The soufflé didn't rise all the way," or "The dog threw up behind the couch."

JACKIE WAS GOOD to the waiter's five-minute prediction. As she came toward the table, I stood up and rushed to embrace her.

"Jackie, what happened? I was *so* worried! Tell me the whole story—you got stuck in an elevator? That's so appalling! What floor did it stop on?" I was rushing my words.

"Oh, Carly, it was *fine*. Everyone was very scared and some of the people . . ."

"How many people were in the elevator?"

"About fifteen of us."

"An elevator man?"

"No, it was an automatic. Some of the passengers got quite panicky, and"—Jackie's expression was bright, almost merry—"I was trying to show them I was calm."

"But *were* you? Weren't you terrified?"

"Not at all. I knew it would be all right. I was like a stewardess." Her giggle was charming and deep-throated. I loved her "nostalgie de la boue."

Jackie had removed her suit jacket. As usual, her clothes were purposely understated (I guess one can make that one of the highest class distinctions)—a mixture of wools, tweeds, and silks, all in beiges, sands, and grays. Her shoulder-length hair was parted on the side and was a darker-than-usual shade of brown. It looked the way it did in several of those candid portraits taken in Hyannis Port— her hair curling with a lovely insinuation of carelessness, as if the photo had been snapped at exactly the right moment, prevailing through even the storms outside.

"Does hair know where its curl goes?" I remember asking her. "Does the curl stay in the same place as hair grows out, even if you have all your hair cut off? Does a curl *know* that at three and three-quarter inches it will bend to the left and then bend back to the right at four inches? Does everyone in the world but me know the answers to these questions?" I went on, "And does Kenneth [Jackie's hairdresser] know the answers, too, and secretly depend on them?" The idea delighted Jackie. Laughing, she motioned to the waiter and in French—a piquant, seductive touch—ordered something with bitters.

I was still flushed from the anxiety that had led me to the bathroom and the Valium. I told her again how amazed I was by her equilibrium in the face of a stalled elevator in a huge office building. Then, throughout our salmon four ways, Jackie and I returned to a subject we'd begun to explore the last few times we'd seen each other, love: its breadth, depth, definition, development, and possibility. For us and others, but mostly us.

One of us, I can't remember who, quoted what our friend the director Mike Nichols said once: *If we can only give up the need to destroy what is good in love, and put aside the need to seek out the new, like Christopher Columbus did, we can end up on our feet.* But wasn't it also Mike who told me during my second marriage, to Jim Hart, *Everything, including love, is political, Carly. So keep the power, keep the advantage. Don't play all the cards?* The conversation—this trying to get to the bottom of the eternal question—seemed funnily like the issue of "curls"! Jackie, like me, loved to figure things out with the benefit of an anecdote containing meta-phors. Or try to, anyway.

By the time we got up out of our chairs, it was almost dark. Before leaving the restaurant, I said my silent *adieux* to the girls on the wall—my dream-selves, my allies. What se-crets, I wondered, did these friends keep between and from each other?

Jackie had a town car waiting outside. It was clear she would at least offer to give me a lift home, just six blocks north. But before she could do that, we were both gustily ushered into the back seat by Jackie's driver, who, in turn, was whisked by the wind, which by now was blowing up from the south and therefore going our way.

Jackie greeted him. "Joel, we're going to Seventy-third and Central Park West, and then we'll continue on to New Jersey." It was when she had a weekend house in Peapack and wanted to get a jump on the Friday night traffic.

Even though Jackie's car seemed modest, it was different from any other town car in which I ever had ridden. Along with being three or four inches longer than other cars, it also had certain similarities to the residence of some imaginary Swiss ambassador. Not a crumb, not a fleck, not a single fluff-end of lint on the seats or the floors or the armrests. It was tempting to conjure up images of chambermaids licking every leathery square inch in one fast, last, lapping touch-up. Much like Jackie's office at Doubleday, where she was an editor, the cars that took her around the city may have *looked* understated, but chances were if you lifted up and peered inside the back seat, you would find a refrigerator and a bathtub and maybe even a reflecting pond stocked with sleepy trout.

Both of us were tipsy, warm, and wet. Settling back against the seat, Jackie pulled the burgundy cashmere scarf down and fluffed her hair, which only managed to redistribute the huge, winking, still-intact snowflakes. I rearranged my own hair, which was and is completely useless, wet or dry. It may sound unbelievable, but I felt, as I had before and would again and again, that at the end of the day Jackie and I were just two girls. Two girls with a few surprising things in common and other things (the most obvious ones) not. Two girls leaning forward eagerly on a late-night dorm room bed, listening to *Sgt. Pepper*, sharing a cigarette and talking lightly, urgently, about love and boys and the people we knew in common, swapping news and gossip and all the other captivating tidbits we just *had* to tell each other. Two girls taking turns on the swings, each of us playing to the other one's material, braced by the sheer conspiracy of each other's company.

Out of the west

Of Lambert's Cove

There's a sail out in the sun

And I'm on board

Though very small

I've come home to stop yearning

Burn off the haze

Around the shore

Turn off the crazy way I feel

I'll stay away from you no more

I've come home to stop yearning

—"TERRA NOVA"

2

An Alliance with a Famous Person Is Always a Dangerous Thing

N O ONE IS MORE INTERESTED in famous people than other famous people. The level of starstruckness among well-known people is deeper, more religious, more out of control. To understand why, one would probably have to consult the courts of Caesar. Yet, even given the truth of the theory, who would ever think that Jackie would be so fascinated? Then again, she was always a reader, a storyteller, a fantasizer, a magic-lover, a romantic. And stories about famous people are most often romantic.

Contrary to what a lot of people believe, celebrity can be isolating. It cuts you off from other people in ways that you're generally late to realize. Understandably, no one to whom you admit this will have even a shred of sympathy for you. The world tells you who you are, and if you start believing those altered versions of yourself, you will grow deluded, transformed, and find yourself hanging out solely with your pet monkey, strangely disassociated from the person you actually are. For some, the only option is to spend time with others who are also suffering to some degree from this unusual condition. In that way you're able to match your experience against theirs, and maybe come to a closer understanding of how phantasmagoric and ridiculous the whole thing is.

I first met Jackie in the summer of 1983, at the Ocean Club restaurant in Vineyard Haven, on Martha's Vineyard. Jackie had bought land in Aquinnah, then known as Gay Head, earlier that summer, and had been busy building her tasteful, sane, and magnificent house on the ocean. Jackie's arrival on the island inspired a lot of mixed, behind-the-scenes emotions. Some feared her coming would change the character of the Vineyard. Who would she invite over to dinner, and who wouldn't she? "An alliance with a powerful person is never safe," my father had told me a few times when I was growing up, quoting the Greek philosopher Phaedrus (his best friend, I always assumed). Yet who would have *not* wanted to meet Jackie, get to know her, see her up close, sit down next to her, capture her attention, maybe even her *complete* attention?

Something in me didn't want to want those things.

Everyone on the island, at least most everyone I knew, was going out of their way to remain calm and unflustered but to still include Jackie in social activities, and there were already plenty of people on the Vineyard in whose realms she was accustomed to socializing: the Marquands, the Buchwalds, the Feiffers, the Herseys, and, of course, the Styrons—Bill and Rose—whom Jackie had known since her college years. There was also a mixture of Kennedy family members and associates, plus one or two of Jackie's post-Onassis friends. Ari had been dead for eight years.

The Ocean Club, where Jackie and I met, was a local restaurant and the energy collector in Vineyard Haven—an ideal melting pot for islanders, located a mere block away from the squarer, more reliable Black Dog. Throughout the eighties, the Ocean Club had a cool, white-powdery, jazzy reputation, edgy yet underplayed, and was at frequent risk of getting busted by the cops. Small groups would collect there for dinner and drinks at 7 p.m., following the club's BYOB mandate with bottles of vodka and rum, equipped with name tags like children's clothes at camp and stowed under the bar counter. After dinner, these same groups would get inside their cars and drive twelve minutes or so to Airport Road, where a nightclub, the Hot Tin Roof, could be found inside an old airplane hangar.

Since 1978, I'd been one of three partners in the Hot Tin Roof, and it had been an immediate success. I can't say why. Sometimes things just work for no good reason, and the Hot Tin Roof worked. The club had live entertainment two or three nights a week, jazz on Sunday afternoons, and dancing all the other nights, with my brother Peter and my friend Tommy Styron as disc jockeys lending the greatest "vibes" to the dance floor. People came there to dance as much as to see and hear the musicians and comedians onstage—Peter Tosh, Delbert McClinton, Cyndi Lauper, Bonnie Raitt, John Belushi, Dan Aykroyd, Rick Nelson, Martin Mull, and Steven Wright, for starters. Even waiting on line gave off a certain twirl and possibility: marriage, babies, nights of bliss, though definitely not in that order.

I had seen John Kennedy Jr. at the Ocean Club earlier that summer, but he'd recently begun bringing his mother along for dinner, wanting to introduce her to a few of the locals he knew and liked, some of whom were busy working at the complex of buildings that was starting to be called "Jackie's house." One day I was having an early dinner there with a well-heeled, martini-drinking group when John came over to our table. He directed the invitation to me: Would I like to meet his mother? I excused myself, aware of being singled out, and took a seat at their table. Trying my hardest not to stare, I told Jackie and John how well they seemed to be blending into the island environment. How was the house coming along? Had she run into any construction problems? Small talk, but our connection felt instantaneous and, for some reason, familiar. Had the weather been conducive to the carpentry going smoothly? Was she already kayaking, even though the water was only sixty degrees?

Over the next few weeks, I ran into Jackie at the Ocean Club a few more times. She was always with her son. "You have to come and see the house!" John said more than once. I had still yet to see it when John came over to *my* house with his friend Barry Clifford, an underwater archeologist who had devoted his life to excavating the *Whydah*, a shipwreck off Cape Cod. I gave John and Barry a full tour, from the basement all the way up to the tower. John seemed to like my decorating style, or "aesthetic," and afterward said to me, "I'd love to bring my mother here. It's so *different*."

In contrast to my Vineyard house—which people who visit describe as something out of a fairy tale, a tilted, crowded, teacup fantasy—when I did visit Jackie's house in Aquinnah, I saw she was likely influenced by her close and most stylishly impeccable friend, the horticulturalist and style icon Bunny Mellon. It was all Nantucket whites and light blues, airy, never cluttered. If I was mad as a hatter, she was as cool as a glass of iced tea.

Everyone on the island wanted to see Jackie's house as it was being built. Someone told me later on that Jackie didn't share John's love for my taste in decoration, but I also overheard the opposite, and that she was especially enamored of my circle garden, where, later in our friendship, the two of us would sit and drink tea or white wine and talk about the various people we knew in common.

If, as Auden said in his poem addressed to Yeats, "mad Ireland hurt you into poetry," then increasingly popular Martha's Vineyard, with all its intellectual vigor and competition, pleasured the summer dwellers into more cocktail, luncheon, and dinner parties than any other place on the map. In a stretch less than ten football fields long and facing the Vineyard Sound lived at least twenty authors, presidents of universities, political pundits, film and television personalities, theater people, and Hollywood producers or writers.

From the island's ferry, their houses appeared to be strung like modest gold charms on a twisted green hemp bracelet. Interspersed among these houses were sundry upper-middle-class homes. Not mansions, but the inhabitants (many year-round) without exception considered themselves most fortunate to just so happen to live between the likes of the playwright Lillian Hellman and the novelist William Styron. In fact, I rented one of those houses in 1980, "the secret house," I called it, to be my "writer's abode" when I was working on an album and the gray sky was dying into the steely winter and the songs were reflecting the oncoming cold.

We were in the eighties—a jumble of old and new blood. The literati seemed to be focused around this mile along the water in Vineyard Haven, where the ferry pulled in multiple times a day. Lillian Hellman's house and garden faced north toward the dock, her rosebushes traveling down a few yards and ending at the water's variable edge. It was a good location for Lillian, as it was for the writer Peter Feibleman, her live-in companion, an author as talented as all the other prizewinning writers who lived on that one-mile stretch of road. Peter inherited most of what Lillian left behind when she died in the summer of 1984.

Next door, down the beach to the left of Lillian's, was the Styrons' beachfront house. It featured a deepwater dock and a famously sprawling lawn on which many gathered for many reasons. The Styrons were Lillian's adored nemeses. A fiercely domineering personality, Lillian was eternally lusting after a worthy competitor. Blushing and flattering, she would often compete with William's wife, Rose (a fine poet and translator in her own right), when in fact the last thing Lillian would have admitted was how deeply she *needed* Rose. It was Rose, after all, who brought into Lillian's sphere many of the quintessentially glamorous figures who spent time on the Vineyard. Rose and Bill were at the center of the Vineyard Haven Main Street elite, which consisted of those "already published" and at the midpoint of their literary reigns. It was a well-established group—brilliant, successful, artistically and politically motivated, and proud to share in one another's leafy, extensive shadows.

Art Buchwald, the resident guru of the island, met regularly for lunch with Jules (cartoonist) Feiffer, Mike (newscaster) Wallace, Robert (dramatist) Brustein, Sheldon (president of U. Penn) Hackney, and John (author) Hersey at the Vineyard Haven Yacht Club (I would often join in for the lobster rolls). I'm not sure what Lillian did there when others were occupied on the tennis courts slamming their crosscourt forehands at each other. But it may have involved sneaking a furtive peek at Rose's calendar to find out who was coming for cocktails that night, leading to a plot to steal Marlon Brando for the weekend when he was meant to be visiting the Styrons.

Lillian spent winters in St. Lucia and New York, so I would know her only during the summer months, mostly on the porch of her house, where she stood imperious, conscientious, and defiant. Her interest in meeting me was connected exclusively to my recent celebrity and 1972 marriage to James Taylor. James and I were of a relatively new breed of kids who had spent our summers on the Vineyard, and in our case returned to establish a year-round life. It was through Lillian that I met Rose for the first time. The three of us were joined one early dinner at Lillian's house by Jane Fonda. Fonda was working with Lillian on the movie *Julia*, which was based on a Holocaust story from Lillian's iconic collection *Pentimento*.

As she cut a healthy bite off her porterhouse steak, Lillian asked, "Is Warren [Beatty, that is] really that good in bed?" Jane and I were supposed to answer in tandem, which, of course, we did, and then, to our utmost surprise and delight, Rose volunteered her own answer. (The things we don't know about Rose might make up a singular category of interest, especially now that she's just turned ninety at the time of this writing!)

Even before I moved full-time to the Vineyard, Rose Styron was talked about incessantly and always in glowing terms. Many people extolled her physical beauty and grace, her poetry, her translations, her relationship to and success in the world of advocacy and social justice. Rose's reputation was well deserved, and I was immediately enthralled by her and by her four children, Susanna, Tommy, Alexandra, and Polly, each one through the years as interesting as they were the first time you had met them.

Bill Styron, Rose's husband, was magnificent—mean and vulnerable and not all that interested in other people except as subjects to write about. He was often ruthless to Rose, mostly because he could get away with it, though no one else could, or would, or ever felt any need to. I met Bill for the first time just before his novel *Sophie's Choice* was published. I remember that the letdown following the huge success of that book and the movie brought on one of his several depressions, made worse by the side effects that go along with taking the wrong medications. It became something of a chore, the delicate, eternally vigilant effort it took not to rub Bill the wrong way and become a target for the churlishness that was a cross-symptom of his personality and his depression.

Lillian Hellman's memorial service (1984) was an underplayed, typically Vineyard affair that took place at Abel's Hill Cemetery, where, two years earlier, John Belushi had been buried. The usual empty beer bottles, dried flowers, and mixed messages of pom-poms and silver skull jewelry had been tossed onto John's gravestone. But it was situated in the same row as Lillian's, and I remember feeling happy that the two of them would be able to socialize with each other in the next life. They would have liked each other immensely. John wouldn't have had any idea who Lillian was, though certainly Lillian would have had a whiff of John's extravagant fame.

Lillian's service was attended not only by the Vineyard Haven group, but also by her close friends from the Mc-Carthy era—blacklisted or not—and others Lillian had collected, in the way an art collector snatches up paintings that might increase in value over time. All of us laughed afterward at a remark that Bill Styron made about Lillian: "We dined together, often on close friends and an occasional deceased writer." Lillian's passing marked the end of the inherent tension between the two powerfully brilliant literary hostesses as next-door neighbors. Something of a letdown for tenderers of local strain and gossip. Although Jackie's arrival a few years before, bringing with it its own quiet force of gravity, might have eased their disappointment.

I WOULD SEE JACKIE again at a party at Rose and Bill Styron's house. It was one of those high-toned, tan-legged, post–*Sophie's Choice*, Chilean-writers-in-attendance dinner parties for which, among their various other heady laureate accomplishments, Rose and Bill were known. That mid-August night, Jackie and I were seated at the same table, one of three closely squashed surfaces holding thirty people in all. It was Rose's way of paying no attention to how furniture should be arranged, or whether or not forks matched up with spoons. It was the apex of chic in a tattered New England way, though authentically unselfconscious, too. As a result, the festivities had a Sunday night pickup dinner sensibility of ease and familiarity, like an impromptu high school reunion in someone's wild and overgrown backyard.

Everyone there that night knew Jackie and me separately. And although Jackie and I had been introduced a few weeks earlier at the Ocean Club and run into each other a handful of times since, we did not yet know each other. The mystery of her, the weight of her history, still seemed nearly impenetrable to me. As I tried not to stare at her from across the table, I found myself entertaining a topic of conversation that might have implied, creepily, that I'd crawled under the table at some point during the evening to study Jackie's feet. During a pause in the conversation, I stammered on the "J" of "Jackie" before somehow blurting out, "Jackie, where did you get those a-a-a-mazing s-s-sandals you're wearing?"

For the first time that night, the focus of conversation was on Jackie, simply and fully. She didn't look at all pleased, either, though somehow I had the impression that it was a "down" night for her in general. As I remember, she left the table and the party before the last course of cheese and salad. Only a few minutes before leaving, though, Jackie answered my question, without flourish or detail.

"I bought them at a bazaar in Pakistan." Her gaze was direct but perfunctory.

"Very exotic," said another guest seated to her right, and Bill Styron said he'd noticed them, too.

"I read about one of your trips, in '62 I think? It must have been so hot and crowded back then." That was Walter Cronkite. Several other guests chimed in, too, and I felt the support and charm of the men at the table as they patched and smoothed the conversation. At the same time, I remember being aware that Jackie, surrounded by familiar faces but also newcomers like me, was in an uncomfortable position, probably not for the first time in her life. How hard it must have been to negotiate being the Jackie having dinner with her trusted friends as well as the "Jackie" from international headlines. I can see how any question posed by someone she didn't yet know, even an innocent one about footwear, might seem like a breach, an attempt to break through into her dark and complex and fiercely guarded history.

MY FIRST AWARENESS OF Jackie—that is to say, Jacqueline Bouvier Kennedy, the very public, very stylish, and always somewhat elusive figure—was back in the sixties, when I was in high school. A scattering of photographs, a collage of opinions, news stories, her all-enveloping walk through the White House. Piecing together my thoughts at the time about this larger-than-life woman, I found, not surprisingly, that most of them centered around the connection between Jackie and her brilliant, handsome husband.

I also remember wondering: How can any woman belonging to the generation between my mother's and mine be so unlike either of us? Had Jackie had to give up her identity completely to become Mrs. John Fitzgerald Kennedy? Was she at the not-so-secret mercy of the Kennedy family? If so, did she come to this realization suddenly, only when she was safe under the covers, jars of Vicks VapoRub and aspirin bottles cluttering the bedside table, faced with a new and overwhelming set of responsibilities, including being pregnant, taking care of the house, and being America's First Lady? I imagined she was not entirely happy to find herself living in so saturating a spotlight. Jackie's own background discouraged anything more public than birth, wedding, and death announcements, though I didn't pick up on all that until much later on.

It wasn't until 1970 or so that the rags began devoting serious attention to salacious gossip about Jackie, now Jacqueline Bouvier Kennedy Onassis. That was a different era, suddenly less oblique and guarded. The marriage between Jackie and the Greek shipping magnate Aristotle Onassis was reported to be on the rocks. The press was leaking more and more details, and the reverence for Jacqueline Kennedy deteriorated for a while into a trashier but still fascinating aura—that of Jackie O. As more information was revealed about Jack and Jackie's past, John F. Kennedy's character and behavior with women other than his wife fell under the microscope. These "other" females posed and sprawled bustily over front pages. They were gangsters' wives, wives of close friends, blondes, brunettes, and some obvious, cleavage-happy Hollywood types.

Facts got twisted and played with. We, the peanut gallery, sat in the far-back seats, adjusting our spyglasses, assessing what we knew, or believed we knew, about the marriage between Onassis and Jackie. I was, like most people, somewhat fascinated. What was she thinking? Why go from universally revered Jack Kennedy to a character like Aristotle Onassis? But more than the facts, what toyed with my imagination were Jackie's reactions to what the newspapers were reporting. How much did she care? How did that concern show itself, or affect her comings and goings with her children? How did she protect them from what were some fairly unlovely details about their father?

For that matter, how much had she always known? Did she have sleuths or spies, or those in her close circle who played both sides? Whether it was the truth or a projection on my part, I felt certain that Jackie was capable of holding a grudge. She would have had to. Did she savor a grudge, love it, roll it on her tongue like a pearl, shifting it back and forth? From the first big hurt until it felt almost irrelevant, just another pearl, slicked over by time but always kept close by. She knew the secrets of the great queens: keeping it all close to the chest. Each fresh, painful image popping up in a dream or on a supermarket tabloid cover just might be rendered harmless, no longer relevant. But these impressions were from a time when I was just a girl who knew Jackie only as a figurine, not yet even a figure, certainly not a person, and some miles and years away from being a friend.

WITH ANY NEW FRIENDSHIP there are moments when another person lets you in, lets you see different notes, moods, colors, shapes. A friendship is like a house in that way. In the first weeks and months, you become meticulously and even overly familiar with the front hallway, the mirror, the hooks, the sneakers and shoes, and the living room, the candles with their black wicks on the mantel. Maybe you go into the kitchen, with its coffee smell, plates, and a bowl recently washed and drying beside the sink. A few visits in, it's now the upstairs—bedrooms, half-opened closets with fast glimpses of belts and scarves, and even the basement with its folded cardboard boxes, the wood stacked up, the window fans and retired kids' toys and wedding presents that never made the cut.

In that way my friendship with Jackie was like entering a stately, vaguely intimidating house, with columns and gardens, a house that showed up in both the National and Social Registers. But I found out that more rooms existed than I would ever have imagined, rooms that kept showing themselves to me over the years. One opened up a few years after we met, when I sang at her daughter Caroline's wedding to Ed Schlossberg. It was 1986.

We were already friends, but not what I was used to in a friendship: close contact, sharing of pain and issues of love and loss. That hadn't happened yet. I sort of understood why she asked me over, say, Pablo Casals or André Malraux. They were dead, but you get my point. I already knew some of the Kennedy family—Teddy, and some of the cousins, Chris Lawford and Steve Smith—I was a part of the tribe who had homes on the Cape/Vineyard, part of the "family-at-large." When Jackie asked me to do this favor for her, I immediately felt that she had become my friend in a different way. I was now in the room where the fire was lit and the coffee was on the stovetop. There was two-day-old fruit compote in the kitchen and no one was at home but us.

In truth, Jackie didn't ask me to sing directly, not specifically, but she did ask whether I knew of any great bands that could play dance music. Just to think of the musicians or poets she might have had access to and who would have jumped at the chance to help, to be at a "Kennedy" wedding, made me so pleased she had enlisted my help. The wedding of John F. Kennedy's daughter. Jackie's daughter. Their only daughter: Caroline.

Caroline, Ed, and I went to see a band called the Supreme Court during a rehearsal at the Embassy Hotel in New York. They were both totally won over, especially by the lead singer, Marc Cohn, who was on the verge of solo stardom. The next thing I knew, Marc, his band members, and I were rehearsing together. The set list included a couple of "just in case" songs I might end up singing at the wedding reception. Caroline and Ed went on to see the Supreme Court at the China Club and got familiar with their music. They called to thank me for introducing them to such a perfect band.

I couldn't get it through my head that Jackie considered me enough of a friend to help with such a significant occasion. I think that was the first time I understood.

THIS, OF COURSE, made it all the more mortifying that I was half an hour late to Caroline's wedding on Cape Cod. Not out of any Queen-of-Sheba complex, but because whoever was in charge of those things forgot to send a shuttle bus back to pick me up at the Kennedy compound in Hyannis Port, where I was getting dressed at Rose Kennedy's house. Since there was no need for me to get to the church early, I hadn't gone with the rest of the family. I had no idea how to get from the compound to the church in Osterville, the next town over—and in a panic I called the local police. In the end, a cruiser driving ninety miles per hour with its sirens shrieking dropped me off at the church.

With a rotating cast of exceptions, Jackie's table was saved for family. She was wearing a very pale green silk cumberbunded dress that skirted her knees. Without the benefit of a concealing midsummer tan, Jackie looked a little tired, dealing with the myriad matters concerning the event, although her eyes were lit with obvious delight at the occasion.

I sat for a while at Jackie's table, along with George Plimpton and a few others involved in the merriment. As was his wont and way and even talent, George was in charge of that night's fireworks display. The night sky was bleary and wet, and George wanted to set off the fireworks before it got even foggier, but the band took a while to get their instruments tuned and plugged in, and we couldn't get ready any faster. I'm not sure if George ever forgave me for making him put on his fireworks display in the coastal fog.

Dinner was followed by toasts from Teddy and cousins one after another. The dance floor filled up fast as the Supreme Court played just the right mix of Stones, Beatles, Bob Marley, Bill Withers. I was encouraged by the lady in green silk to kick off my shoes and go up there and sing with them. I did without any of my usual nervous fluttering about. Marc and I sang "Chapel of Love," "Is This Love?," and "Lean on Me." Jackie made a motion that I should do a song of mine. I sang a few of my self-penned or -recorded songs: "The Right Thing to Do" and "Nobody Does It Better." Out of the corner of my eye, I saw Arnold Schwarzenegger standing at the edge of the dance floor, looking as though he was wondering which of the guests he was going to crush between his two fingers. Teddy came to the stage and asked the band to play "Jump." Marc asked, "Which 'Jump'—the Pointer Sisters' or Van Halen's?" The senator obviously didn't know the difference, hiding his ignorance with a smile. "Just 'Jump,'" he said, walking away toward Arnold.

After the band went off at the end of the night, Marc approached Jackie and thanked her for giving him the opportunity to play at Caroline's wedding. Jackie responded: "Yes, it's just like a day at the fair!" Everyone was happy. It WAS like a fair. Except one of us was wearing the most beautiful short-sleeved wedding dress and looked particularly spectacular.

A FEW WEEKS after the wedding, Jackie called me. As an executive editor at Doubleday, one of her job responsibilities was convincing famous or interesting people to write their autobiographies. On the phone, Jackie told me that she thought my life would make a "fascinating" story. Yes, I told her, but there was that "but," followed by a second "but."

I was all the things one might have imagined a person in my position to be: immensely flattered, feeling not up to the job, and worried about being honest—of course about my parents, and especially about what I would have to leave out, the *nucleus* of the story, in fact, which was my mother's long, adulterous, secretive relationship with my younger brother Peter's tutor. After a month or two of phone calls, and me coming up with various excuses, and Jackie coming up with other, gentler angles—"You could just concentrate on your relationships with different people: your mother, your sisters, you and Mike [Nichols, the film director, a mutual friend], and, of course, James and your kids!"—I finally told her the truth.

I couldn't tell the story of my family, at least not yet. It was too sensitive, and too soon, and my mother was still very much in the land of the living. I came back with another idea, a story about a bear whose daughter wants to be a dancer. A children's book with, I hoped, an irresistible appeal. A book about how a daughter turns unwittingly into her own mother would be both universal and (I thought) sweet at the same time. You can't go wrong with bears! Bears almost never lose! The story had more detail than that—though honestly, not a whole lot—and soon enough my talented illustrator and artist friend, Margot Datz, and I met up in New York at Jackie's office at Doubleday.

As other people have noted through the years, Jackie's office was extremely modest and filled with nothing but her charm and her books. A few months later, we met there again to go over the formal agreement for our book, which now had the title *Amy the Dancing Bear*. In an effort to be businesslike, Jackie said, "Do you have a lawyer you'd like to talk to about a contract?"

I'd considered this dreary possibility, but finally I said, when we were alone, "Why don't we do it ourselves? We could draw up something simple—just us—and not terrify ourselves with the amounts of paper we would have to stay up nights worrying about." By that point, I was already willing to give her everything. I was at some place of consciousness where it mattered only what she thought of me, rather than the other way around.

"Yes, I like that approach, and that means we could get to work on it right away."

I said, "What about twenty-five thousand dollars up front, which I can share with Margot?"

"That sounds very reasonable." Jackie showed not an ounce of anything but innocence as she went on: "I don't know any more than you do about the business part, so good, let's wing it together!"

"That sounds terrific." I was nervously pleasing her, though the money we'd just agreed on *did* seem fair to me. More to the point, I didn't know what the hell "fair" was, and just wanted to be in the right ballpark. Jackie would know if an amount was reasonable or not.

Amy the Dancing Bear was a success, which is why it felt quite natural for me to write a second children's book. After all, over the years I had told enough bedtime stories to my children, Sally and Ben, and they were all stored in my head, awaiting further embellishment: an aunt here, a brother parrot, a snowman from Brazil.

A year or so later—shortly before our lunch date at Café des Artistes—Jackie and I were on the phone, talking about my follow-up book, *The Boy of the Bells*, a Christmas story scheduled to be published the following year. The question came up again.

"What do you think would be a reasonable advance?" Jackie asked me on the phone. "Have you thought about it at all?"

I, the perennial people pleaser, proposed the same amount I'd come up with the first time.

"What was that deal?" Jackie asked. She said she couldn't remember.

"I got twenty-five thousand dollars up front, and I split it with Margot."

An audible breath came through the receiver. After a thoughtful pause, Jackie said, "Oh, Carly . . ." Another pause. "You got *screwed*."

All of a sudden, I was given a glimpse of another Jackie. *I* was the one who had made the offer—or had she? When we had agreed on that figure, the two of us weren't really friends yet. If anything, in that moment I realized how cheaply I had sold myself. In retrospect, Jackie had done the normal thing, protecting the interests of her company. After all, she was also a businesswoman, someone who I later found out traded in her own clothes at Michael's consignment shop on the Upper East Side and walked away with cash for new ones, and who in exchange for getting the best price on whatever seized her fancy at Tiffany promised to give the salespeople's business cards to her more international friends. No, unlike her new friend Carly, Jackie was familiar with the concept of *worth*.

"Screwed?" Really?

The itsy bitsy spider climbed up the water spout

Down came the rain and washed the spider out

Out came the sun and dried up all the rain

And the itsy bitsy spider climbed up the spout again

—"ITSY BITSY SPIDER"

3

Mike

WHY DID JACKIE AND I connect as deeply as we did? I've thought about it a lot over the years and tried to analyze it, but I'm left only with theories. We began as acquaintances, fellow islanders with people in common. We then developed a professional relationship that quickly evolved into something more casual. I came to believe that, to Jackie, I represented normalcy, relief, a kind of freedom. Most people, even some of Jackie's good friends, saw and treated her as separate and impossibly lofty, a person who couldn't be teased apart from history. Around me, Jackie may have felt more like she could be herself. Just possibly, she found in our friendship the comfort and solace a hostess feels when a high-stakes dinner party is over and she can change back into her unironed housecoat or sloppy jeans. From almost the very beginning, Jackie and I were fortunate to inhabit a bubble of ease, that thing that pulls you in for the long ride. The sense, even, that you and the other person have "been there before." Where the comfort is automatic.

We also had a shared ability to let our thoughts dip into the magical. Our imaginations took flight in similar ways. We both loved "The Night Before Christmas" and everything it promised, those nighttime moments when you hold your breath to hear a hoof on the roof, the moment when everything seems possible, and life and its complexities have yet to be revealed. "Wasn't that what so much of becoming an adult was?" I remember asking Jackie once—the innocence of belief we're born with slowly getting replaced by the pained recognition that nothing and no one are really as they seem? *Was* there magic in the world? I believed there was—I *knew* there was—and Jackie did, too, but to admit that in polite circles put you squarely in the categories of "child" and even "lunatic." So what?

Jim, my second husband, had a theory that my being more of a "crazy artist" than any of Jackie's other friends helped her get closer to her own emotional life. I won't ever know for sure. I do know that Jackie was, in her own way, very artistic. Her generation was crowded with many women from a certain background who would have no sooner gone into a career in the arts than jumped off a mountain. A life in the arts was too showy, too insecure, too *not us, dear,* except as it may have played out after a sherry or two in their fantasies at dusk. So, instead, their lives became performance, and they became social performers: fresh flowers on all the tables, paintings hanging on the walls, beautiful wardrobes, a desire for harmony and balance playing out in the day-to-day spectacles of life, at cocktail and dinner parties and after-school events that they—these artists who never called themselves that—orchestrated before dimly appreciative audiences who also never called themselves that. It was only when their children or grandchildren happened on a set of immaculate ink drawings, or a design stenciled on a vest, or closets dark with gypsy dresses and sashes that no one had seen their mother or grandmother wear, that they realized who and what had been pushed aside and kept under wraps.

If you're not an artist, at least not in your job title, who or what can help bring out that side of you? I think on some level Jackie savored the incoming and outgoing tides of my life, my nervous system acting out scenarios that became hers, too. But it was always at a remove, like a book borrowed that you never expect to be returned.

Perhaps Jackie and I were two halves of something similar, mine exaggerated, hers in need of greater encouragement. At the same time, how different she was from me, so refined and horsey and Newport-y. That pillbox hat! Even Chanel went beyond my field of vision. I was droopy earrings and imported Mexican heavy cotton dresses, guitar by my side or piggybacking my shoulders. I could never be as sylphlike and straight-backed, or as cultured, in that European way, as Jackie. My idols in the world of fashion would somehow slyly and slowly converge with Jackie's until, by the accident of a few movies, Audrey Hepburn would bridge the gap.

Early on, we shared how much we each reminded the other of Audrey Hepburn. For me, Jackie was the Audrey Hepburn of *War and Peace* and *My Fair Lady*. For Jackie, I was the Audrey Hepburn of *Funny Face*. I wore the *Funny Face* black turtleneck and ballet slippers look, while she was the very incarnation of Audrey's final persona in *My Fair Lady*, as perfect as if she were created by Henry Higgins.

Despite this meeting-up of likenesses and differences, I do know that for the ten years Jackie and I saw each other regularly, in New York and on the Vineyard, if I didn't call her for a while, I could be sure she would call me. Whether we were at her office at Doubleday, discussing what word should go where, or being in contact during her illness, Jackie was always there for me, just as I was for her. Our conversations were punctuated by her laugh, which would start out high-pitched and light before descending into something full-chested that touched the bottom octaves.

"You know one of the reasons you're intriguing?" Jackie

said to me early on in our friendship. "It's because you're a *Thoroughbred*."

She explained that I was refined, highly tuned, though sometimes a little too edgy for my own good. *Of course* I was afraid of performing in public, Jackie said; in fact, I *shouldn't* perform live, ever! "I'm a *workhorse*," Jackie continued. "Big feet. Flat feet. And part Belgian. A cousin of mine used to call me 'Suffolk.' I think it was a brand of draft horse he was familiar with."

Being someone who was and still is tortured by my own getaway energy, I decided to believe her. At least the edgy part, the wearing of my anxiety like an escutcheon, though very obviously she was exaggerating her role as the foil, the clopping, intrepid horse that could power through any storm with its gaze fixed and its mane lowered.

"Don't you wish sometimes you had a little bit more of one thing, and a little bit less of another?" I asked, shifting the stream of the conversation. If a seismologist ever took the time to measure my own emotional graph, I told Jackie, he would see lines and squiggles going up and down at levels so fast and precipitous he couldn't possibly capture them.

"Oh, Carly, you have the temperament of an artist. It's why Mike loves you as much as he does. Because we all know you're on the edge of falling off the stage, of losing control..."

From the beginning, Jackie's and my discussions about

working together on a book were peppered with high-school-type gossip about the people we knew. In that category, the most brilliant person in the room—the subject worthiest of interesting, eternal conversation—was Mike Nichols, the actor, director, screenwriter, and producer. Mike, who began his career as one half of Nichols and May, who went on to direct Broadway shows and movies such as *Who's Afraid of Virginia Woolf?*, *The Graduate*, *Carnal Knowledge*, *Silkwood*, *Heartburn*, *Biloxi Blues*, and *Working Girl*. Mike, who'd won more Emmys, Tonys, and BAFTAs than anyone, not to mention an Academy Award and a National Medal of Arts. Mike was our smartest, wittiest, most brilliant link, the man whose attention and approval we both craved. He was a magician in the way he could arouse and prohibit desire simultaneously. Every time Jackie and I met for lunch, or for tea, or for an ostensible "business meeting," the subject always turned back to Mike, his dazzlingly present absence connecting the two of us in the same way Mike and I would so often circle back to Jackie.

We weren't alone. Almost every woman I met during the 1980s who knew Mike was besotted with him. He was Tiki Zeus—the nickname his wife Diane Sawyer suggested for him during a game a group of us—me, my husband Jim, Diane, Mike, and our kids—played one Thanksgiving at an inn in Vermont. We went around the table trying to answer together the question for each of us, "If our parents hadn't given us the names they did, what would our 'real' names be?" Mine, voted on by the group, was Theodora Dance.

I'm not exaggerating when I say that Mike was the pre-
liminary conduit to Jackie's and my friendship. At the time,
Jackie had a vision of me as someone "Mike" knew, and who,
therefore, was acceptable. What's more, whenever I talked
to either Mike or Jackie, I knew that each of them would
milk me for details about the other. If it seemed sometimes
that the conversation Jackie and I were having was about to
end or stall, our breathing would naturally bend the air half
an octave, our conversation jogging ever so slightly before it
picked up on its high-octane topic: the mutual fascination
that Jackie and Mike had for each other.

Looking back, I have to believe Jackie was just as uncertain about herself when it came to Mike as I was. Why
else would we both keep casting our eyes to him for his approval? It might have been less confusing and more straightforward for Jackie to allow that, yes, Mike loved both of
us, so we must *both* be worthwhile, no? I know this is an
oversimplified explanation, but the attention that Jackie be-
stowed upon me was often hard to separate from the specter
of our mutual friend, who compelled and perplexed us in almost equal measure.

Did we think Mike was afraid of his own artistic soul?
Why did he fall in love with the women that he did—his
first two wives; Gloria Steinem; his third wife, Annabel
Davis-Goff; then Diane Sawyer? Diane was a breathtaking
presence and one whose intimacy I sought. She was brilliant and dazzling. Still, I never felt as close to her as I
wanted to, and could never bring her and Jackie together.

What abiding effect did Mike's alopecia since age four, resulting in baldness, have on his need to succeed in high society and the worlds of celebrities with houses on warmer islands, the colorful places that build the nightlife pages of *Vogue* and *Town & Country*? Did it have something to do with Diane? (Jackie thought maybe it did, though Mike explained away Jackie's bristling tension around Diane as "a younger woman thing." After all, at the time Mike and Diane were married, Jackie was close to sixty, and Diane wasn't yet forty-five.)

I could relate to all this intrigue, and still feel out of danger. I was just a foil, a minor player, there to move the plot along, though whenever I told Mike bits and pieces of the conversations I'd had with Jackie, he ate them up like a rich dessert. *This reflects badly on me*, I wrote in my diary, *having to tell [Mike] but mostly not keeping the confidence of one of the most impressive women in history*. It was an ongoing problem for me where Mike was concerned: seducing him with information, always fearing he'd see me as dumb or confused, then berating and hating myself for engaging in such a low form of entertainment. Mike had a taste and an eye for the amusing out-of-character things our friends did and once pointed out that he'd bumped into Jackie on the street and she was chewing gum. As the two of them chatted, Jackie didn't stop the motion of her jaw, or bother to tuck her gum behind her teeth. She kept chewing. I wondered: Was gum-chewing a kind of épée-thrust on Jackie's part, a reminder that somewhere in her heart there lurked a tough and fearless street kid?

The president of my record company said to me once: "I wish you wouldn't hang out with Mike and Jackie and Diane so much. You need to hang out with musicians and lose the image of being so exclusive." I suppose he was jealous, too. Who would imagine, if they were thinking clearly, that Jackie Kennedy Onassis lacked soul? That Mike Nichols or Diane Sawyer or Jim Hart or Mike's collaborator Elaine May or others I hung with lacked soul? Please. Was he suggesting that his new collection of hit makers were the only ones with "soul"? And how did he know who I was hanging out with, anyway?

MIKE AND I HAD MET for the first time on Main Street in Vineyard Haven, in front of Leslie's Pharmacy. He was visiting Lillian Hellman for the weekend. Lillian introduced the two of us, and in the same breath told us that Mike's and my children were going to marry one another someday. At the time, Mike was married to the Irish writer Annabel Davis-Goff, and had two beguiling, out-of-the-ordinary children, Max and Jenny, who were exactly—almost to the day—the same ages as my children, Sally and Ben. A few months later, I would sit next to Mike at Susanna Styron's wedding, and we would stand together the next summer at Lillian's funeral.

For the next ten years, as our partners came and went, the Nicholses and I were an extended family, spending all our holidays together. Before they married, Mike and Diane stayed in my guest cottage when their house just down the road was being renovated into a showplace even more spectacular than it was when the actress Katharine Cornell had lived there in the 1940s and '50s. In my own Forrest Gump–like life, my parents had taken me to visit that very same house in 1952, when I was a child, to pay a visit to Ms. Cornell.

Mike's and my friendship grew, becoming creative in 1985 when he asked me to work on the film version of Nora Ephron's novel *Heartburn*, starring Jack Nicholson and Meryl Streep. Working on that film was a labor of immense love and appreciation—it was difficult to imagine anything better—even though the movie was based on Nora's book, a pretty liberal depiction of the breakup of her marriage to Carl Bernstein, whom I also knew quite well. Told from Nora's point of view, the book and film are both somewhat unsparing of Carl, other than Jack Nicholson being a great choice to convey Carl's charm and intellect.

Once, during lunch at the now-defunct Mortimer's on the Upper East Side, I filled Jackie in on the backstory. "Mike and Carl met for lunch at the Russian Tea Room, and Mike told Carl he was planning on directing the movie version. Carl felt terribly betrayed, but I guess Mike told him that 'art was art'—only a lot more cleverly and eloquently than that, I'll bet. Anyhow, on the way out to the street, the two of them had a physical altercation of some kind in the revolving doors. I always pictured them getting caught in the same position, face-to-face, unable to move. Air running out. No running water!"

Jackie commented that many artists became distant in the course of doing what they had to do, no matter what their medium happened to be. I confessed to her that the whole thing made me slightly uneasy, too, especially when I considered writing the music for a film that took sides against one person I knew for the sake of another. "But I'm writing the lyrics to the theme song from Nora's point of view, so whatever I end up writing will be from *her* perspective." I told Jackie that Nora had written down a few phrases to help me get deeper into her character. "She gave me 'burn the soufflé' and 'kiss the host good-bye.'"

At the end of the movie, the Nora Ephron character leaves the Carl Bernstein character, flying off with her children to New York once it's become clear that her husband has been unfaithful for a while. As the plane takes off, the Nora character sings "Itsy Bitsy Spider," her hands demonstrating to her daughter the motions that match the words to the song. I knew that was a good taking-off place for me, too, and I remember sitting at my upright piano on the Vineyard, writing out new chords to "Itsy Bitsy Spider." Nothing revolutionary, mind you, just taking a few liberties here and there. And, even better, Ben and Sally and their little cousins were just at the age—between eight and thirteen—where they knew and could sing the song.

Mike's and my professional relationship continued throughout the eighties. In 1989, I was in the middle of recording an album when Mike asked if I'd be interested in writing the score for another film he was directing, *Postcards from the Edge*, starring Meryl Streep as Carrie Fisher, or at least a likeness of her, a drug addict going through rehab. I sat down at the piano one day with a cigarette, some pills, and a yellow pad, and by nighttime I'd come up with a new song called "Have You Seen Me Lately?," which became the album's title. It got Mike's stamp of approval, and also made my husband, Jim, cry when he heard it. I made a demo so that Meryl could get familiar with it, as it was written for her to perform. Throughout the making of the album of that same name, the song "Have You Seen Me Lately?" went into the movie, then out, then back in again, changing singers and adding or subtracting various piano parts.

Jackie, I remember, was so fascinated by all the machinations taking place on the movie and sound sets that she asked me to give her a daily report. "I called Meryl and sang it over the phone to her and Meryl told me she loved it," I told Jackie, "though later Meryl told people she didn't think she could sing it. She was too intimidated. In fact, Meryl is a *terrific* singer, and I wrote the melody with her voice in mind."

But all that would come later, when new people arrived

into Mike's life and mine. Mike's marriage to Annabel ended in 1986, and two years later he married Diane. During that same time period, I met and married Jim Hart. The good news was that since Mike and I had one of those relationships that expands rather than shrivels up when someone new comes in, the four of us made a perfect quartet.

Jim and Mike were just beginning what would be their own long, devoted friendship. Diane had grown up a church-going Protestant and was always kind, respectful, humble, and careful. The exception was that when she was in competition for a juicy interview, Diane would leave her rectitude on pause. At the same time, there were always little clues scattered here and there that I could never quite decipher. Whenever I'd call their house, apartment, or hotel, and Diane answered the phone, she and I always chatted a few minutes and then she said, "I'll give you to Mike," before handing over the phone. But what about Diane and me? I wondered. Was Diane only putting up with me for Mike's sake? In general, though, I remember the delight and comfort we all took from the great nights, lunches, and vacations the four of us enjoyed together. The gifts Diane sent me during the first two or three years the four of us traveled as a pack were so grandly thoughtful as to be almost embarrassing.

ONE NIGHT, during one of the two summers when Mike and Diane were staying at my guest cottage on the Vineyard,

I gave a party in my gazebo, which overlooks the field where the sheep, donkey, and horse grazed in bucolic un-selfconsciousness. (They still do.) The day had been hot, and it was still warm at dusk when I began serving margaritas and tacos. That morning, when I was talking to Jackie on the phone, I told her about this little get-together and—naturally—invited her to come. I was surprised but thrilled when she said yes on such short notice.

But as the night went on, it became clear I hadn't accurately taken the temperature of the relationship between Jackie and Diane. There was, at the very least, a sophisticated tension between them. Over the years, Jackie had said a few witty, disparaging things about Diane, and while I took in the wit of Jackie's words, I was mostly blind to the negativity at the center of her feelings that was, as Mike had intuited, competitive. Just maybe, in the wake of Diane and Mike's marriage, Jackie thought of Mike as the man who got away.

As usual, I could relate to it all, while still being a spectator, out of the crossfire, should there be any. I felt very close to all three of them. Though, if truth be told, my strongest allegiance was to Jackie, who I felt truly let me in, whereas Diane could be chilly, practiced, and untouchable. I've come to believe that Diane is as shy as I am, but that she hides it successfully behind language and upbringing. If truth *really* be told, I could just as well have been a foil for all of them. Jackie! Mike! Diane!

The night of the party, all the other guests had arrived except for the major players in the coming drama. At last they began to appear. Mike came across the lawn from my little guesthouse—the Black Honeymoon Cottage. He came alone, as Diane was taking a little extra time to summon her grace to face Jackie, who also had yet to show up.

I was seated on the wooden bench that lines the circumference of the gazebo when my peripheral vision caught sight of a figure moving in slow motion around the circle garden, blond hair obscuring her face. Equidistant, and going at almost the exact same speed, a brunette, also alone, was making her way with casual determination past the pond on the opposite side of the gazebo, observed only by me, the sheep, the donkey, and the horse. Up the stone path to the steps came the brunette, head held high, eyes steady and bright. I still have lopsided dreams of that double image. Betty and Veronica dreams. Dreams of magnificent, treacherous girls.

The gazebo is laid out so that there's no way to enter it other than along a single stone path. For a few moments, it looked as though Diane would reach the path just before Jackie. I was convinced Diane must have seen Jackie and was timing her entrance so as to avoid one of those awful "comedic" moments when two people crash into each other. Jackie got there first, Diane arriving maybe ten seconds later, thanks only to a contrived, diminished stride.

The others—there were maybe ten of us there—greeted both of them, standing, shaking hands or delivering their kisses cheek to cheek. The air zigzagged with overly zealous compliments. I watched closely as Mike maneuvered the force of his eye contact toward Diane, except for a single, barely perceptible blink, where it was clear he'd taken in the entire political performance of the two women. I remember Jackie's straight back becoming straighter, Diane's neck modestly bowed, swanlike, her head to one side, smiling, as she accepted the wreath of the underdog.

wah wah be doo dah

zop wah de doo dah

wha wha wha de do bop be do

za be do da

—"UNCLE PETER"

4

Daddy and Uncle Peter

OW DO YOU PINPOINT the occasion when a friendship begins to take hold? Do you know it when it's happening? Did it begin with the small notes, sometimes regarding the book we were working on, that Jackie had begun sending me in the mail and that I would answer, leading to a lively written correspondence that was sometimes accentuated by a thoughtful gift? Did our shared respect for and adoration of Mike make us more like sisters? Did it inspire our realization that we both were influenced by powerful fathers? Powerful in Jackie's case in that she adored her father, "Black Jack" Bouvier, and powerful in my case in that I felt pushed aside by mine—Richard Simon.

Had Jackie grown up with the confidence to be plucky or shocking and deserving of love, whereas I turned to one man after the next to find someone worthy through whose eyes I might see myself as lovely or brave and safe? (Then again, I'm fairly certain that show business is overflowing with people who fall into the "rejected-by-their-father" category. If you can't get the love of the first man you meet, the love of a million people isn't enough.) Jackie had won the competition with her sister, Lee, whereas I grew up feeling like I ran in eternal third place behind my own two sisters, Lucy and Joey.

As a child of six or seven, when my stammer was full-blown and my front teeth were sprawling across the universe that was my mouth, my father may have looked at me as a caricature. I took advantage of this perspective and encouraged his artistic eye to envision me as a character in a Jerry Lewis skit or perhaps even as a hitherto unknown, recently born Marx brother. Whatever the reason, he began to take pictures of me, and not just of his more beautiful daughters and his wife, Andrea. I knew that, compared to them, I looked silly, and I responded by posing like a big silly clown. In those photos I look desperate.

"Daddy, please look," I'm saying. "I won't try to be pretty

for you, but I *am* funny. Can you see that, Daddy? I'm *funny!*"
Or, more likely, "I hope I'm funny."

When Daddy never seemed to look back with any appreciation, I went further into my pent-up, abstemious, closed-off affect, which probably worsened his attitude toward me. I thought I was the only human who could get their feelings hurt.

The story I tell myself was that I grew up with a father in name only, a third daughter, the only one born with the Semitic features he thought he'd left behind in some foreign country. Yes, Daddy was a king of a father to my sisters, Joey and Lucy, whose looks and bearing were almost Prussian in their bladelike fineness. If it weren't for Uncle Peter, my mother's brother, who distracted me from the uneasiness I always felt around my father, I'm not sure how I would have survived that painful part of my growing up.

Thank goodness for Uncle Peter! Uncle Peter, who taught me chords on the ukulele, who sang, "Yes sir, that's my baby" on the porch of our house in Stamford. He, with his brother Dutch, started a band when the two of them were stationed at Fort Dix. Peter played anything that Louis Armstrong could play, but better in one unusual way—all the sounds came directly from his mouth, with no horn in between. It was naughty, lively Uncle Peter, the epicenter of joviality, who laughed me around kitchen and dining room tables and up and down the seesaw of life. Uncle Peter, into whose hand I slipped my own during Father's Day in pre-kindergarten, my other hand gripped loosely in my father's, which felt so alien.

As Uncle Peter tilted into old age, his eyes might have lit up a little more slowly, but he was still gorgeous, still laughing, still delighted by life, an aging autumn poplar a beat or two less wild in the wind. When he died, I was desolate. Uncle Peter felt like my *real* father, the Daddy who genuinely loved me, and whenever I look for warmth in men, I always expect it to have the face of Uncle Peter.

Jackie was so taken with the stories that had entered our conversations that when he died, she asked about many more details of his life. Particularly, she loved the story that at his funeral there were at least seven women who introduced themselves to me and, with a wink and a nod, revealed that they had lived in my apartment on Thirty-fifth Street from time to time. At LEAST seven, all either Cuban or African. They would circle the room and come back to talk about him some more. Uncle Peter's wife was a fine, upstanding woman. I'm sure she would not have approved of these Murray Hill luncheon trysts. Even Peggy Lee (whom Peter had managed) told me she had visited the Murray Hill apartment a number of times as well. She made no secret of the fact that she was very involved with my uncle, my own version of Black Jack.

"Uncle Peter has always sounded so much like my own father," Jackie said once. "Isn't it just like us to meet at that transit, the crossroads of role models?"

I wondered: Had I spent my life idealizing, glorifying,

and chasing after the absent male? During the final days of my first marriage, I remember thinking that James looked at me as a man might when regarding a faded flower that he had once picked and now, with difficulty recognizing the beauty for which he picked it in the first place, discards it. It was a feeling that Jackie, apple of her father's eye, would probably never know.

A few years before Uncle Peter died, Jackie was intrigued enough to want to hear his albums, so on a late afternoon I went to 1040 Fifth Avenue, following an explicit request to bring some of his music. It led to one of the most intimate conversations we ever had. I had made a cassette, my most favored form of copying music. It was easy to pick out ten of my favorite Peter "Snake Hips" Dean songs. By then he'd made four solo albums with a pianist who was also a great friend, Buddy Weed. He'd never imagined that there would be a demand for live shows. Who would have guessed he'd hit the road at seventy-three with a band? He played the ukulele and danced while he was playing.

I arrived at Jackie's apartment at 4 p.m. It was a Thursday in early 1989. I was about to go to Florida for a midwinter vacation with my husband Jim, Jake Brackman (my collaborator and close friend), and his girlfriend, along with Sally and Ben and their friends. From there, it would be out to L.A. for the Oscars. I had been nominated because of Mike—because of my song "Let the River Run," in the movie *Working Girl*. I was terribly depressed and had no conscious reason why I was, though depression had been my frequent companion, called by many different names through the years. I had wanted to ask Jackie about depression, knowing she had suffered that awful disease, probably accompanied by post-traumatic stress disorder, but I left it alone for now.

Marta, Jackie's housekeeper, answered the door. I'd walked across the park and wore a heavy coat that my friend Marsia had made for me. I felt like Anna Karenina in it. It was long, to the ground, lined in burgundy-colored cashmere, with a trim that resembled snow on a lamb's fur. Jackie and I talked about the coat and about how we both loved Russian style.

"Have you read Troyat's biographies of Peter the Great? Of Tolstoy?"

"I love the Tolstoy biography even more than the one about Catherine the Great, which is saying something, as I thought that was going to be my all-time favorite book."

"What about Stefan Zweig's biographies?"

I don't know which one of us said what, but it was another example of our shared taste in and passion for reading. She later gave me a book about four great Russian palaces, a big volume containing plates of interiors and exteriors of these Russian national monuments, and suggested that if I needed some good decorating hints, I should study them. It was the kind of witty remark that I would expect and want from her—from anyone who knew my taste, really—but particularly Jackie, with whom I shared a love of certain styles, although, given her general penchant for understatement, not others.

After my coat was taken, I sat on the couch facing the museum side of Fifth Avenue. Jackie was on a chair with her back to the view.

"Did you bring it?" she asked.

"I think it's our lesson for the day! Yes, shall we put it on right away?"

"I think we may have to remove the rug."

"We'll be dancing tonight!"

Marta asked if she could watch, and we clapped our hands like toreadors for some reason, after which she announced the option of "sherry or port or tea or coffee."

"It's not that kind of music, Marta," I explained. "It's my uncle Peter!" I was very proud of him.

"Shall I put the tape on? Any particular song?"

Marta went into the kitchen, soon returning with a large pot of tea in a Russian samovar, with glass cups. There was jam for sweetener.

The tape started with "Baby Won't You Please Come Home."

"What a lovely voice." Jackie noticed Uncle Peter's gentle tenor delivery and his rhythmic rounding off of the notes.

She just listened and sat still.

Then came on "Four or Five Times," a duet with his niece, me. Its tempo got us both up. It was as though a Spanish dance troupe had just entered the room and we were its partners. All three of us started dancing independently of one another. Jackie asked Marta to turn the volume up. Then Uncle Peter broke into a scat section where his voice was the trumpet.

"How does he make that sound?" Jackie asked with a note of incredulity. "That is something I have a feeling no one I've ever known would be able to do."

"Here, I'll show you." I closed off my throat and pushed the air through a small space left for just that purpose. Maybe you could use that space for other reasons, such as swallowing gnocchi or something slippery with a little sauce, but it certainly worked well for making the sound of a jazzy muted trumpet. Then came a great song of James's that Uncle Peter wanted to record: "Don't Let Me Be Lonely Tonight."

"I don't know why I decided to include it. Probably just to suffer a little bit." The conversation paused, and we allowed it to. Then I looked up and past her, out the window to Fifth Avenue, where the sun had shifted and the clouds revealed a more golden afternoon. Contemplatively, Jackie evoked a frequent and resonant topic:

"What makes it love?"

We continued on as if engaged in a musical duet.

"How does it know?"

"Is it different in some countries?"

"What is the difference between like and love?"

"Does love always include like? Does like always include love?"

"What are the symptoms physically, if any?"

"Is it altogether different if it's lost its luster and maybe its lust?"

"When love is required, can there still be lust?"

"How long can it maintain its name: LOVE?"

"If you have to think about it and try to give it a name, is it already in a category that is unlikely to be love?"

We weren't exactly Thomas Merton or Saint Thomas Aquinas or Saint Augustine, but we were trying. Trying, as most people do, to pin it down. I remember that day, talking. We were so consumed. So happy to be in each other's company, trying to figure things out. I thought of the story she had told me once of her father, Black Jack, running around the reservoir in a black rubber wet suit. We laughed. She told me about the scent and softness of the fur coat that Janet, her mother, wore as she leaned over "little Jacqueline's" bed before going out for a glamorous evening. It was a vivid memory. She told me that JFK's favorite song was "Greensleeves." That grandfather Bouvier, a mayor, used to take extremely hot baths followed by freezing ones. That there was tremendous fear of poverty in the family. Jackie was born three months before the 1929 stock market crash.

We talked about James and the stubborn repetition of his rebuffing me. It was as if once he'd arranged his attitude, he was damned if he wasn't going to live up to it. Rejecting me. It had to have made Sally and Ben very conflicted about how to feel, not only about their parents but also about themselves.

"How would I get over this?"

"Would he be able to soften?"

"More tea, please!"

"Yes, a little sweetener."

"I mean," and I kept underlining my point, "how is it that James, who is so brilliant, doesn't know that the more you push someone away, the more opposing force happens, the more attack and passion it has? The yang makes the yin retreat. However, when the yang makes the yin retreat, if the yang goes too far (ha ha ha), it makes the yin go yang!"

Jackie took a minute to unravel my Dr. Seuss–like sentence and make a sound that was more giggle than laugh but also more breathy and more trebly than bass-y or guttural.

"I certainly believe I know what you mean."

I continued:

"I remember the first time I felt as if I was a germ to him. At first he was still uncertain how to respond to me and didn't quite know how to behave, but then Kathryn [Walker, actress and James's second wife] showed him the way. Kathryn made him scared. He followed her whims; he was such a good boy. He never wanted to visibly disobey. I'm sure it was the beginning of a buildup of fury that turned into rebellion against her in the end. She was so threatened by his past life that he had to work overtime allaying her fears, principal among which was his relationship to me and Sally and Ben, not to mention his entire life on Martha's Vineyard. His detachment has been an ongoing misery for all of us."

Jackie was appalled, but her reaction was muted. After

all, she'd been hit about as hard as one could be and come out alive. And then there was Ari.

She told me about how Ari made excuses when he began to see Maria Callas in secret. He'd say he had to go to England for a conference of his tanker builders. She smiled broadly, and three syllables of laughter later had conveyed that he wore a lot of cologne when he was leaving to go see Ms. Callas. As if it would last a "stinky ride" on his plane for six hours.

"If she was going to meet him at the airport, I mean, he could've reapplied it. I think he wanted me to know I wasn't everything to him. He didn't want to leave me completely— not entirely, in case I turned into the ideal mate he hoped he'd married."

Jackie told me then about the period of her life when she was her most vulnerable, when, for the sake of her children, she had decided to take refuge (if only it had turned out to be that!) with Ari, whose power and wealth seemed, at the time, like they might make life bearable. Or at least possible. Everything was for her sweet children, to keep them safe.

That evening was a turning point, a new room in the house of our friendship revealed to me, one in which we could roll up the rug and dance, even amid the wreckage of the past.

I'm the most dangerous person in this room

The way you look

I could do some damage to myself

—"EASY ON THE EYES"

5

The Laughing Garden

SOMETHING ALWAYS HAPPENS to me on Memorial Day. We all know that Memorial Day is a day to honor those who, as Abraham Lincoln said, "gave their lives that the nation might live." I realize, respect, and am grateful for that, of course. But for me, Memorial Day is also and always a day on which something goes wildly awry. One Memorial Day weekend, a violent and jealous woman threw a bottle of brandy at me, grazing my forehead through the back window of a limousine, when I was making a gun-moll getaway with her husband. Another year, I was visiting my best friend and lyricist, Jake Brackman, standing a foot away from his kitchen stove, when a bolt of lightning came in through the window and burnt a perfectly round hole in Jake's copper teakettle. Dramas like these never occurred on Abe Lincoln's birthday or on Arbor Day.

The Saturday before this *particular* Memorial Day weekend, in 1986, once again I was visiting Jake, who lives about an hour and a half outside Manhattan, in Hudson. I took the train from Grand Central Terminal, on the Hudson River line. The route is spectacularly well conceived, winding its way northward with almost continuous views of the Hudson River Valley and the river itself, through Ossining, Peekskill, Garrison, Cold Spring, Poughkeepsie, Hyde Park, Rhinebeck, Claremont State Park, and finally arriving in Hudson.

After spending two wonderful days at Jake's house—a huge, magnificent, fallen-apart mansion with deep, dark wood staircases molded by Calvert Vaux and a kitchen that was in the middle of being noisily renovated—I decided to return early to New York on the Sunday morning train. Jake and I pulled up at the Amtrak station with only a few minutes to spare, and I stood in line behind a very tall man waiting his turn, as I was, to buy a ticket. "*Jim!*" Jake called out suddenly, in his commanding voice, which in this moment had a slightly ironic, maybe gangster-like tone. And the tall man turned. It was as though they were co-conspirators in a bank robbery, though I later found out they had met only a few times before. Even though it was Memorial Day, there was no blip or click in my brain, no instantaneous recognition or prescience to alert me that I was standing across from the man I would marry.

"Jim, this is Carly. Carly, this is Jim."

Somehow, despite Jake's unmistakable vowels, and Jim clearly hearing my name, I would find out later that Jim thought I was Linda Ronstadt. I turned toward the ticket counter while the two men caught up, but just then the train arrived. Jake picked up my bag while Jim said his good-byes to the family members who had dropped him off—people whom I would get to know later as his ex-wife, Alannah, and young son, Eamon.

I boarded, and made my way to the last car, which was empty. Before the train left Hudson, I opened my book and began reading. A moment later, the pneumatic door slid open, and the tall man whom I had just met (was his name Jim?) looked down at me. Had Jim maybe said anything to Jake about me, similar to the "He's *major, major!*" that Jake hissed into my ear as he and I said our good-byes?

"Would you like to sit here?" I said, not entirely sure how hospitable I genuinely felt.

He would if I didn't mind. "Train's a little crowded." Good, he had a sense of humor. I liked that.

He positioned his overnight duffel bag on the overhead rack, hoisting my tiny doll's luggage beside it to make room for his rangy and expansive self. The high reaching of an arm, the slant of a hip, the split seconds of eye contact, Jim's body settling unselfconsciously into the seat across from mine, my own legs and arms crossing and folding—the exciting awkwardness of two bodies sizing each other up, as if responding to some unseen wind. Then . . . nothing.

I didn't start a conversation. He inspired silence in me. Not the silence I fall into when I'm tired or bored or awed. A new kind. At one point, I looked down at his shoes. They were leather, a relic from the 1970s, the kind of shoes for sale in arty stores in Cambridge, San Francisco, Boulder. His feet made a pleasing swelling shape against the soft leather edges. I next snuck a peek at his knees. They were elegant and roundly pointed and seemed longer than most, as though the tendons, ligaments, and bones had conspired in unison to prepare their owner for a life of aristocracy. If these knees were to show themselves to full effect to various chirping country maidens, they would require a full schedule and season of polo, kilts, high socks, and *Howd'youdooo's*!

Jim was also extremely well-spoken. Some people have great presentation, others great content. Few mix and match the two as he did.

I would write in my diary:

Jim Hart, who I met on the train, told me tough stories, and I revealed some of mine (fewer). I told him as we pulled into Grand Central that he could ask me some questions. We had a little laugh about that.

A few months later:

Somewhere during this week, I began falling in love with Jim.

Soon after that, as I sat on the porch in Menemsha, the up-island fishing town where I had a little cottage that looked out over the site of a concert I was about to perform for HBO, I wrote:

Jim and I have been in constant contact talking over our possibilities and carefully becoming more intimate with each other over the phone. Jim had a talk with Jake yesterday, and Jake allowed there were quite a few problems Jim would face in loving me but that I was well worth all of them. Jim is so many surprising things, many things in the right amount.

As an aspiring theologian, Jim had been expelled from a Franciscan seminary due to that tricky vow of celibacy. Now in his thirties, he had a day job selling insurance, but he really wanted to be a writer, a novelist, a poet. His friend William Kennedy, who wrote *Ironweed*, which had just won the Pulitzer, was acting as a guide and mentor. Jim was now also a recovering alcoholic, and since getting sober had become something of a star sponsor to many members of the recovering younger set in New York. But nothing that I knew of his background foreshadowed what we would face in our marriage. And in the beginning at least Jake was right that, worth it or not, I would be the bearer of problems. Soon after we were married, I was forced to think that one of my biggest problems would be my own snobbery.

When did I become such an arbiter of my own taste? I wrote in my diary when, newly married, Jim and I had spent a long weekend at a rural "ye olde" New England inn. *How did I decide I was better than other people at knowing what good sheets were? What would Jackie do? Call a maid? A doctor? A friend nearby with a mansion?* As compensation for my own psychological unease, my bodily comfort had always been of paramount importance to me. I was a careful, hyper-aware stenographer of my smallest pains, trying to pin down any and all unexpected tremors and twitches, sneaking inside myself less like an interested explorer than like a tiny frightened kitten: *Why am I feeling so strangely flushed? Was it the dinner that made my stomach hurt? Was there fish shit in the water? Is the barometric pressure making me so spacey?* I wondered if Jackie worried about such minute sensory fluctuations as these.

When exactly had I turned into Howard Hughes? Jim's and my long weekend at "ye olde" inn was a challenge: How much external stimuli did the two of us need? Could we be alone together for seventy-two hours, minds and bodies existing side by side, without the usual diversions of phones, TVs, and assorted other electrical devices? Weren't we supposed to love this back-to-nature, roughing-it, long-weekend vacation that, of course, cost me a small fortune? Darn right we were! So why wasn't I having more fun? Had I forgotten how? Why did I need at least a week to practice depriving myself before entering an actual sensory-deprivation tank?

Nothing worked for me. The bedsprings didn't yield evenly, at least not in any of the right places. The curtains wouldn't close properly. The pillows were lumpy, like floating pockets of fat, evoking what I imagine is stored in the backroom refrigerators of plastic surgeons. For the first time, I noticed how absurdly paranoid I was about the sexual history of the hotel bedspreads and throw pillows that remain on the bows and sterns of beds, unlaundered, for months on end, a sexual guest book signed by countless Debbies, Pauls, Judys, and Scotts. Jackie would have at least stripped the bed and called someone with a starched white apron.

When Saturday morning came, a scent crept up through the spaces in the floorboards, one that turned into a *smell*, then an *odor*. It was rancid bacon grease. It infused our bedroom, coating the bedspread and the ratty curtains and suffusing me with a melancholy made worse by Jim's indifference, the faint lift in his eyebrows signaling his dawning awareness that he was married to a princess who had uncovered what was surely only the first of many peas beneath her mattress.

"I can't stand this smell," I told Jim, making a joke about

my own hothouse-flower sensibilities. In response, Jim basically told me to get over it, the implication being that he and I were going to be smelling rancid bacon grease for years and years and years, at least until death did us part.

Jim's unconcern about the smell, his shrugging acceptance of imperfection—burnt coffee, diners with loud voices, kitchen doors that thumped open and shut—upset me maybe more than it should have. Our olfactory organs are completely different, I thought. That bacon smell was confirmation, maybe, of just how bourgeois and spoiled I was. *Was* I those things, or simply accustomed to high standards around my own comfort in ways Jim wasn't?

In the end, maybe, it was all about nature, and how humbly you carried your human self in its presence. New Yorkers regularly sought to domesticate nature and go for glamour. Unspoiled men like Jim found this idea impertinent. Of course, this war was not just between city and country, but female and male, clothed and naked, wood and stone, showy and plain, each party saying to the other, "You just don't get it," and both being right.

The bacon smell receded, but how could it ever be forgotten? Over the next few years, Jim would tell me what a perfectionist I was, what a burden it must be, how it must spill over into all aspects of my life—my surroundings, my looks, my work, my friends (they had to be the smartest, the funniest, the profoundest friends in the world), and, of course, Sally and Ben, who were growing up in their very own category of *perfect*. I would try to justify my existence by telling him it went hand in hand with being an artist, despite the fact that most of the world's great artists weren't what you'd call neat freaks.

But the differences between Jim and me seemed more minor than all the things I loved about him. He had proposed to me in the fall of 1987, and I said yes. A few days before Christmas we were married on the Vineyard in a small ceremony, our very short honeymoon spent across the sound on Nantucket during a Doctor Zhivago–ish blizzard. By then Jim had already met most of my friends, and he and I became an established couple at New York and Vineyard lunches, dinner parties, and birthday celebrations.

I could tell that Jim's presence in my life fascinated Jackie, inspiring both her genuine curiosity and her fierce and growing protectiveness. Once I remember telling Jackie that my mother had instilled in me the belief that it was more thrilling for a woman to save and set free some poor, starving artist than it was to do the conventional thing of marrying a man for security, or status. My mother also, perhaps contradictorily, told me that men preferred "little women," i.e., women who were physically on the small side, as it brought out their protective instincts. (Unfortunately, I got tall—too tall—very early on in my life.) I think most of the men I got involved with saw me as a mother, someone who wasted no time in giving too much right away, with my wide smile and my body saying, *Come in and I will protect you and never let anyone hurt you, don't mind me if I lose myself along the way.*

Was I at risk of making the same mistake with Jim? We had already come to an unofficial agreement: Jim would quit his job selling insurance and devote himself to writing his novel and being a good stepfather to Sally and Ben, and I would happily support both of us because at the time I could. Naturally, Jackie, and no doubt everybody else around me, took eagle-eyed note of this. Jackie in particular worried that maybe I was being taken for a ride. Based on conversations she and I had had, I knew she had an old-fashioned philosophy of love: the man takes care of and supports the woman. Jackie and I also had different ways of thinking about money or, rather, joint marital resources. I was more share-and-share-alike (or maybe, deep down, I felt that a man's love had to be bought). My feelings on the subject weren't exactly uncomplicated, but Jackie was adamant: *Carly, you will never respect a man who doesn't take care of you.*

She put it even more bluntly. "You will come to find lots of faults with Jim if he doesn't get a job pretty soon," she said at one point, sounding a lot like a mother, though not mine. "How long must you do this to yourself?" My mother was enchanted with the idea of the poor, starving artist, while Jackie preferred them *after* their commission to paint the official portrait of Charles de Gaulle.

Here is a diary entry from not long after we got married. Jim and I had had a fight. I was willing to apologize, but here is what I wrote:

I'm unable to stay still. Making beds, lighting candles, worrying, imagining things, soaking up every last ounce of pain. Checking myself to see if I'm looking all right, attractive enough for your re-entrance. Am I too unhappy? Will I look too anxious? You can only notice or see real knowledge of other people by the little expressions that cross their face when they can't control them. When they don't know they're being noticed. Not the ones they bring to a party. He'll notice mine. My grimace of disapproval, my mistrust, but more than that, my basic lack of the spine that would hold my back straight and sure if I could control all of these little postures of self-worth. And then . . . yes. My empathy. I always see your side too. What's with that?

You stay away. Maybe on the street, maybe a pizza with the "crowd," maybe a dark corner with a cigarette and one friend. I need you bouncing fierce, courageous rabid, making my need whole. Pinning me with kissing and losing it like a first date. Like you don't know the outcome. You can't wait. Urgent like a tribal ritual, on the front of the beat revealing impatience. Maybe someone in a tent is on their deathbed.

You are the quiet soldier, trained that way, or cold. No dancing tonight. Only coolness of fakery. Forty-nine degrees. Your passion is for something else. How could you anyway have passion for something so barely at a simmer, already cooked and waiting on the stove for hours?

"Jim is not for you, Carly. He's got to get a life," Jackie told me. "He's handsome and charming and yes, he can talk to Mike and he can be a comfortable best friend in your circle, but if he doesn't get a job, you'll end up despising him!"

Meanwhile, my mother complained about his grammar. "He speaks like a gangster." I corrected her: "No, Mother, that's the way they talk in the seminary."

Jim believed he didn't have to exist in the material world, that love could be completely spiritual. I let him believe I agreed with him, when the truth was that I secretly also craved cars and emeralds! For his fortieth birthday, I surprised Jim with a Mazda RX7 convertible. Was I showing him by example what I wanted him to do for me? Whenever Jim brought home a trinket for me—a little thrift-shop cross, for instance—I gave him the most gripping, exhaustive hug possible. *Jim, how could you have brought me such a beautiful piece of jewelry?* I would say, aware of how over-the-top I sounded. No doubt I would have praised to high heaven a shredded triangle of napkin from the roadside restaurant where Jim had eaten lunch that day.

"Of course you wanted a car," Jackie said when I told her how I felt. "A gold thing or two. And you say the poems and the songs were substitutes? No. It doesn't feel like that to me, Carly. It feels like they are the *currency*. They are your *birthright*," Jackie went on. "Every woman wants to be serenaded, the way James serenaded you once. Jim writes poems for you. It fills that same need."

I can't remember Jackie's exact words to me over the years about men and women—but I *do* remember their heart, their meaning, their message. This was the general gist:

Women are passively persuasive because for centuries we had to depend on men. And of course they have to be men. Especially the short ones! (I can hear her laugh.) *The short ones stand up straighter, which only ends up showing you how short they really are! And we—women, that is—think we want to get into a romance with them. We cast them, or they cast themselves, as the great ones, the ones who can rescue women. Rescuing women until they're blue in the face. Women, in turn, are forced to be the ones who get rescued—that is, if they agree to play that part. And women want to give men what they want— to help them feel like they're playing their part even more. So you do that—and then you become more like a garden. If you're strong—and you are strong, Carly—you will want them to be strong. And you will want them to show that strength in different ways.*

Men need to conquer. They're bred to. Unless you let men be the ones who bring home the food, they will resent you for not letting them play their part. And they will step on you.

Jackie could hold her face as still as a marble statue for minutes on end. The only break in focus was a very slight movement in one eyebrow. It was always a giveaway of an emotion that practice and technique kept in line. When I didn't respond to the last part, at least as it related to Jim, the flinch in her brow put an end to the conversation and the subject. Did Jackie feel like she was barking up the wrong tree? At a loss for how to respond, I simply acknowledged her words with a big, ambiguous, up-and-down motion of my head. At the same time, I thought, She's right. She's spot-on, even. If I insisted on having illusions about love, illusions that would inevitably end up getting doused by the cold waters of real life, I might as well be married to a pretty funny gardener who tended me, nourished me, and wrote poetry to me—the satisfied, constantly laughing garden.

No doubt sensing I was vulnerable to getting taken advantage of, Jackie was also very protective of me around my other friends—or rather, the people I liked to *think* of as my friends. In the early nineties, during the preproduction of *Romulus Hunt*—a family opera Jake and I wrote together—we hosted a combination reading-and-singing that was not open to the public. It was an intimate event, with the audience gathered in a half circle around the stage. Jackie was there, sitting very close to the stage next to the Irish writer Edna O'Brien. Edna was my favorite writer. I worshipped her talent.

I first met Edna at a Christmas party Jackie threw in the late 1980s, and we became fast friends. Later, Edna stayed with Jim and me for almost a month in our New York apartment, and I even turned my office into her bedroom. Edna also stayed with us on the Vineyard. Edna especially adored Jim, relating strongly to his childhood (it was one of those

Irish-Catholic connection things), and in turn, around Edna, Jim became more confident, and more confidently Irish.

He was particularly funny around her because Edna was so particularly great an audience for him. Having an ear and a wit, hers is a writerly mind. She listens extremely well and asks a lot of questions, and her writing has always been a Japanese garden of strange, bucolic, wondrous turns. You can tell she is tucking everyone's words away somewhere, answers that will come out of the mouths of half-real, half-dreamed Irish men and women in novels she will someday write. On the Vineyard, I always remember Edna hard at work, writing things out on a yellow pad, occasionally peering out of another room to ask, "Do you think this word is right?" She could also be extremely seductive. She would sit very close, and place one of her hands on you like a cat paw, while occasionally perhaps unconsciously purring aloud.

Once Edna threw a party for me in London, and the following night I met her and Sasha, one of her two sons, for dinner at a Chinese restaurant. I think Edna was hoping to fix me up with him. When I was married to Jim, it's funny how many people made a point of trying to fix me up with other men, as if they intuited things about Jim I couldn't see or understand. Just maybe they spied an opening!

It seemed as if Edna and I had had a long, intimate familial history, which is why I was so surprised when I got home after the reading of *Romulus Hunt* and Jackie called. After dispensing with some very flattering *oohs* and *aahs* on

Jackie's part, I made the obvious comment that she'd been sitting with Edna. "Yes." Jackie stopped. In her soft voice, she said, "Carly, Edna is *not* your friend." I asked her what she meant, and Jackie told me Edna had made some not-very-nice remarks about the music and libretto.

What did I do after I spoke to Jackie? I called Edna up the next day. I wasn't concerned I might get Jackie into trouble; Jackie was untouchable, and Edna would never have dared challenge her. Edna denied everything. She told me she'd loved the show, that it was charming. She assured me she lacked the vocabulary even to describe an opera—*that* was the issue here, she said, nothing else—and she had no idea how Jackie had even gotten the *idea* she disliked it.

It didn't feel divisive, Jackie telling me this, or competitive. No, it felt specific to Jackie. She was the only person in my life who could ever have said that. I was typically apprehensive about the opera, and no one else who knew me would have wanted to put even a single negative thought in my mind. Jackie had no idea I would turn right around and call Edna, and I never told Jackie I did, either.

I recollected and then checked on some gorgeous, memorable descriptions Edna had written. Just one of thousands of them, referring to Joyce in her biography of him: "He entered the social order of Ireland as a deliberate vagabond." Now, that's my cup of tea. It didn't occur to me that when Jackie warned me about Edna's friendship, there might be jealousy around. Maybe Edna thought I had lots of money and wondered, bewildered, how her considerable artistry could be less lucrative than mine had been?

Of course, I have had many friends with whom I've had all-too-human misunderstandings. There have even been periods of time when there's been a chilling chasm filled with silence and resentment. But the great majority have passed into the good feelings out of which they were born.

During that same phone conversation, Jackie said, "Do you know who your friends are?"

We went through the list, person by person. There was her, Jackie, of course. And Mike. The list went on. At one point, Jackie brought up Jann Wenner's name. Jackie and Jann had come to know each other when Jackie's son, John, was launching his political magazine, *George*, and looking around for editorial wisdom. "Are you friends with Jann Wenner?" Jackie asked. When I told her that I knew him socially, she said, "Well, watch out for Jann Wenner, too."

The only thing at the time I could think of was the 1985 film *Perfect*, with John Travolta and Jamie Lee Curtis. Jann and I had both made cameos. Jann, who plays himself in the film—that is to say, the founder and editor in chief of *Rolling Stone* magazine—and John, who plays a journalist, are eating lunch in a Manhattan restaurant when I come along, recognize John from something terrible he wrote about me, and toss my Bloody Mary at him. I remember Jann kept screwing up a very simple line of dialogue. He got so flustered, he missed it again and again. This went on and on, for five or six takes. Every time Jann messed up his line, John had to wipe Bloody Mary mix off his face and change into a new outfit so we could reshoot the scene.

Since then I'd run into Jann once on the Vineyard and again at the wedding of mutual friends. Until Jackie said, "Watch out for Jann Wenner," I had no idea there was any bad—or embarrassed—blood between us. Then again, year after year, I have been overlooked for the Rock & Roll Hall of Fame. Now, I know Jann is not in complete control of who gets inducted, but rumor has it he can be vehement about keeping certain people out. Almost everyone else in my "peer group" *is* a member. Of course, there may be other obvious omissions, but none, I have to guess, where a Bloody Mary may have been involved!

Nostalgia you fake, you bitter sweet ache

The time that you take could make another

    heart whole

Could the truth be I won't really see

How much I love you

'Til it's over

—"WE JUST GOT HERE"

6

Bring It Back
to the Center

THERE WE WERE THE FOUR OF US (Jim and me
and Mike and Diane) having dinner at Mike's apartment at the Westbury Hotel. Two couples. Carefully
prepared food, rich conversation, wit and ease. Mike always
making the others at the table feel they can't go wrong,
whether they're at their cleverest or stumbling worst. The
two women at the table—Diane and me—in love with their
men, and vice versa. And by "in love" I mean the dynamic,
visceral, passionate love that newness enhances and exag-

gerates. The kind where you can't believe it, *you still can't believe it*. How you *ever* attracted someone with such immense qualities!

What's more, Mike and I were ecstatic with each other's good fortune in finding such perfect mates. About Jim, Mike said to me, "How can someone look so good and have all those smart things coming out of his mouth the way *he* does?" In response, I said in my genuinely pleased-beyond-reckoning voice, encouraging immense happiness, "Well, how could *anyone* have the poise and glamour of Diane, and she's not missing anything that I can see."

Superficially, as I said, it was flawless. It's astonishing how in polite society, even the kind that pretends complete naturalness and the most casual jousting, people can mask their sexual jealousy. The women (Diane and I) were giving each other so many loving looks and nods, warm glances— the paraphernalia that makes up "the big front." Neither of us was being insincere. It was just that whatever it was that gave rise to the positive smile, or the appreciative laugh, held also a modicum of pain.

A woman in that particular phase of her love doesn't *want* another woman to be wonderful. I couldn't help but imagine Jim at some point gazing at Diane, delighting in her beauty, originality, and overall loveliness. Just knowing the threat exists tends to dethrone another woman. At least it does me, I admit it. And those feelings are extremely unacceptable. When another person loudly appreciates a member of the same sex, it's almost always underscored by a desire to find the flaw, commit it to memory, then clothe this deviant and pathetic envy in praise of sculpted cattiness: *She is so beautiful and talented—I just wish I could manage to be so detached!*

In his novella *The Death of Ivan Ilyich*, Tolstoy touches on the relationship between Ivan Ilyich—"an intelligent, polished, lively, and agreeable man"—and his servant, a peasant boy named Gerasim. Gerasim is the only person in Ilyich's sphere who shows compassion, authenticity, and no apparent fear of death. Mike and I had both read and dissected the story, but at the time I never anticipated that at some point Mike would begin to project a similar dynamic onto Jim.

Their friendship was about true, genuine love between a younger man (Jim) who had no material or professional expectations and an older man (Mike) who was surrounded by and weary of people who did. Once Mike and I were talking on the phone and his other phone rang and he said, "Oh, god, I hope it's going to be a *we* and not a *them*." I hoped that I was in the first category—that I belonged to "we." Maybe what was gently growing between Jim and Mike, that I believe never blossomed, was their mutual attraction. I was so damn innocent about men, particularly the ones I'd already agreed in my small head were heterosexual. Having complex sexual feelings was within the limits, but my formative (and, it turned out, very narrow) idea about love was from an image in the Golden Book *The Happy Family*: the pie on the stove, the dog barking, Mommy and Daddy holding hands, the screen door slamming.

I didn't think for a moment that there might be a spoken or unspoken hint of sex between the two men. Mike and Diane were as apparently "unswinging" a couple as I'd ever known, and I certainly never had any inkling that Jim would come out a quarter century later as gay. Not bisexual, but really, really preferring men. Without any doubt at all. Over the years, these sublimated shadings would only reveal themselves arduously in strange, strangulated ways.

Unforgettable is that day in 2004, years into our marriage, when I raced in a beating heart of a car over to Mike and Diane's house, and blurted out like an insensitive Roseanne Barr, "Jim's *gay!*" Mike's Oscar Wilde–ian response: "Oh, not him, too." Mike gave me hell for that, and for all that followed my revelation. His front was: "How dare I discuss Jim's sexuality with anyone, or at least with him?" Diane proved more supportive. She turned out to be so much more than I'd ever imagined in a variety of ways. Sometimes she just needed an opening line.

WHETHER OR NOT THE COMPLEXITIES inherent within our relationship were already there, Jim's and my marriage didn't get off to an easy start. Two or three years into things, as Jackie had warned, I was becoming more and more resentful about Jim's bank account, or rather his lack of one, and also about his hesitance to take responsibility around the house.

To ask him to participate didn't seem outlandish: I wanted Jim to pitch in, help out, feed the animals, do the dishes, take out the garbage, buy toothpaste, *take part*. I felt ungracious for even thinking these thoughts. I told myself that if Jim were helping pay our monthly expenses, maybe I wouldn't have expected as much on the domestic side. One day I wrote a list entitled *What I Need and from Whom*. Jim, of course, was first. "For him to get a job," I wrote. "To contribute financially to our marriage. To initiate more. To provide thoughtful romantic gestures: Gifts. Flowers. 'Let's go out to lunch.' 'Let me take you to the . . .' *Let's*. I want him to say *Let's*. Beyond basic needs, there's no 'let's.'" Then I would remind myself that Jim's more accessible qualities—his intelligence and talent, and my respect for both those things, not to mention the need to be near him—were more vital to me than whether or not he put his bowl in the dishwasher or hammered a few nails or brought his sneakers upstairs to the closet.

Against an ongoing backdrop of money squabbles and silent, mopey resentments, our disagreements were simply ways of distracting ourselves from what was really going on. There was a big fight late that summer when the Rolling Stones brought their Steel Wheels Tour to Shea Stadium. Jackie had told me that John and Caroline wanted badly to go, and almost timidly asked if there was any way I could get tickets and maybe even sneak everybody backstage. Well, I was always happy when Jackie asked me for anything, so of course I would do everything I could to oblige her! Jackie said that John played "You Can't Always Get What You Want" night and day on his "player."

The night of the concert, John, Caroline, Ed, Jim, Ben, the great beat poet Allen Ginsberg, and I piled inside a big, white stretch, and an hour or so later, flashing our backstage passes, flew past the guards and roadies and into the general, all-purpose eating-and-socializing room. I was nervous Mick wouldn't come out before the Stones took the stage, as I knew how much John wanted to meet him, or so Jackie had hinted. I understood. As a mother, I would have done everything I could to make sure Ben wasn't shunted aside if he was ever in the presence of one of his idols.

In the end, Mick made a brief, slinking appearance in the room, and proceeded to make an immediate beeline for John. It was like a summit meeting between two of the world's most instantly recognizable romantic and sexual magnets. It didn't last all that long, and I don't know what they talked about, but when the concert was over, and Jim and I were back at home and getting ready for bed, Jim suddenly lashed out at me.

"You were obviously flirting with Mick. It was embarrassing, and dumb, and you looked like a groupie. And you made me look like some feckless hanger-on."

"I was flirting with Mick? Jim, I didn't say one *word* to Mick!"

"Since when do words count? You didn't need to *use* words!"

"Jim, this is *insane*. Is this some projection on your part?"

Our argument was maybe less about Mick than what Mick symbolized. My romantic and musical history, for one thing. But also cars that dropped you off at VIP entrances, and backstage passes, and the unnatural closeness to all the illusory goodies and lures that that sort of life holds out, of which not a lot of people get to partake. I was one of those fortunate people, and I regularly reminded myself of just that, especially during some paroxysm of shame or arpeggio of self-hatred or period when my records weren't selling and I felt like a complete failure. No, compared to most people, I had it awfully good.

It was two years into my marriage that "Let the River Run," which I'd written for Mike's film *Working Girl*, won a Grammy and a Golden Globe, and was nominated for an Academy Award for Best Song in a Motion Picture. Since I had already won the Golden Globe, I knew that I stood a fighting chance for the Oscar. But instead of excitement or glee, I fell into a very familiar abyss.

In an effort to deal with my nervous system, my mood swings and depression, for years I'd been taking one tablet after another, one promise after the next of potential relief, escapism, *deliverance*. These pellets almost never gave me what I wanted: a meaningful, momentary "out," a lowering or even hushing of all the clatter and volume filling my brain. Nonetheless, for years I'd excused myself and slipped away to the nearest bathroom, as I'd done a few years earlier at Café des Artistes while waiting for Jackie to arrive. I'd unbutton my medicine bag and choose.

Which one would it be? Did I want a Sinutab sleepiness, a Benadryl spin? Did the answer lie in what a friend had brought me from overseas—Veganin—or did it require a big, stomping intruder like Xanax? Then Prozac came along, a breakthrough to the mainstream. A "cure for depression and anxiety"!

The first time I took Prozac—a mere chip of a single pill—was in 1989, a week or two before Jim and I embarked on a trip to Florida, a pre-Hollywood vacation, in a rock 'n' roll bus outfitted with six bunk beds and a reckless, terrifying driver named Boots. I had just spent that wonderful evening sharing Uncle Peter's music with Jackie. Sally, Ben, their friend Jed, Jake, and Jake's girlfriend, Lila, came with us, too, through Charleston, South Carolina, where we ate a crab dinner, then on to Savannah, Georgia, where I'd booked us all hotel rooms.

The answer is that they have yet to invent a pill strong or dexterous enough to offer me a sufficient safety net during the two weeks of torture I experience before boarding an airplane. Once I board a plane, sit, click myself in, and very publicly ingest a Xanax or a Klonopin or a Valium, along with a swig of gin, I'm silly and relaxed (because who wouldn't be)—but that's all aboveboard and, as a result, much less interesting to me. For various reasons, my preference was to sneak pills—a sliver of this, a crumble of that—and to be alone with that delicious, underhanded *knowing*, as if I alone was the keeper of a colossally interesting secret that I wasn't about to tell anybody.

The doctor who put me on Prozac advised me to increase the dose slowly. But the more I took, the worse I felt. Much of the time during that trip, in fact, I was wishing life would go away for a bit. By the time we got to Palm Beach, the last stop before we headed back north, my depression was so extreme that I began (doctor's orders) increasing the Prozac, and a day or two later I was taking a whole pill. In Palm Beach, I remember sitting by myself most of the time drinking piña coladas and reading the Alcoholics Anonymous "Big Book." I found it incredibly helpful, as nothing else I'd ever read zeroed in so well on the merciless fixation human beings have on finding something, anything, "outside the self." Some *thing* that satisfies the craving for God, for relief, and mercy, and centeredness, and Mother, and Father, and infinity, and safety, and peace—peace that also *lasts*.

Jim and I got back to New York with only one day to pack before we had to leave again for L.A. and the Oscars. But what I would have to do to get to the West Coast stood

in my path like a rushing river stocked with snapping croco-
diles. I thought about doing what I so often do—disappoint.
The fear of flying, the fear of such a public event, it just
seemed like too much. As long as I was reading the Big
Book, I felt sane, but whenever someone tried to talk to me,
I tensed up and turned into an actor playing myself. I spent
the next twenty-four hours listening to "affirmation" tapes
I'd made, including ones I'd even asked Sally and Ben to record. "Mommy, you are big and strong and beautiful, and
you deserve this honor of being nominated for such an in-
credible award. Winning is not necessary. You are great anyway. You are *safe*." Imagine being so frightened that you are
compelled to ask your barely adolescent children to mother
you. I was that desperate. Despite taking a whole Prozac
every morning, it felt hard enough just to exist. All I wanted
was to sequester myself—to eat nothing, say nothing, do
nothing, be nothing.

To my surprise and relief, the flight aboard the Fox corporate jet—a Citation, or a Gulfstream—was uneventful,
assisted considerably by my travel mates, Mike and Diane,
my managers, John and Brian, and, of course, Jim. Diane
was especially fun and helpful, and she and I chatted the entire flight.

Once in L.A., at the Hotel Bel-Air, we were given the
most sumptuous suites imaginable. Jim slept in a separate
room. He and I decided that for that night sharing the same
bed wasn't necessarily an asset, as I would likely be tossing

and turning and trying on different shades of eye shadow. The day before the night of the Oscars was Beauty Day. Harry Winston minions appeared, bearing assorted diamonds for me to choose from. I took a long Hollywood bath, and then had a massage. Along with the Prozac, I swallowed three Percocets (yes, a major drug reserved for the Oscars) and half a Valium, my plan being to delay taking the other half until thirty minutes before the program got under way. I dressed in the pantsuit that my friend Marsia Trinder (who made clothes for Mick and other rock stars) had made especially for me, and spent the next hour applying my own makeup. When anyone else does my makeup, hothouse flower that I am, my face gets bloated and red and feels like swarms of red ants are crawling over and under it.

The stretch showed up promptly at 4 p.m., and Jim and I, Mike, Diane, Melanie Griffith, and Don Johnson piled in so tightly that our knees collided. When we reached the Shrine Auditorium and the red carpet, I was functioning very much like a robot in the company of other well-programmed robots, funneled into lines in front of microphones. I tried to answer questions like "How do you *feel* about tonight?" while the crowd screamed out the names of stars as they entered. It was dizzying, but the most interesting thing that took place during one of my answers—"It's just so unexpected . . . but of course I'm extremely honored"—was my sneaking the remaining Valium half from my pantsuit pocket and into my mouth while simulating the removal of a stray hair from between my lips, somewhere in between the words "unexpected" and "but of . . ."

As we entered the auditorium, I felt both manic and extremely afraid. Shaking, and walking closely behind Jim and John Sykes, my manager, I spotted Max von Sydow in the aisle. Although I had never met him, for sheer diversion's sake I tapped him on the shoulder. "Max, Max, it's me, Carly. I just wanted to remind you that in that movie you did with Liv Ullmann, I played the *tree*." It killed a couple of minutes, and Max von Sydow was a gentleman who never let on that he thought I might be in my cups, or the pharmacological equivalent. Or maybe he thought, Which tree?

The award for Best Song was the evening's first award, and Sammy Davis Jr. and Gregory Hines presented it to . . . me. Of course, it came upon me as a "complete surprise." I stood up there and gave the credit to others, and was somehow focused and quietly effusive. Especially toward Mike. My God, so many of us owed such a huge debt to Mike for whatever success and glory was handed us—and he, in turn, was so incredibly proud of all of us. I thanked Jim for the contribution he had made to the writing of the song, which was sometimes literal but also spiritual.

I felt so "out of this world," I told Jackie afterward, and she went on about how wonderful it was and how proud I must have made Mike. She quipped, "You poor thing. You must have had to carry that statue around all night, from party to party, wanting to show it off, but instead (knowing you) contorting your whole body to keep it out of sight."

After that night, my depression didn't return for a long time. It may sound unreasonable, transiently hopeful, and fairy-tale-like, but for the first time in a long time I felt *no* depression whatsoever. Was this testimony to my core hollowness? Was it refutation of the widely agreed-upon belief that happiness is supposed to come from the inside, *not* the outside? Even when my mother called the Hotel Bel-Air later that night and said, "I'm so proud of you! Look at all those people who deserved it more, but *you* got it!" her words didn't knock me off my pedestal or cause me to slump back in the south-facing direction of old agonies. I passed the comment off as her obvious envy, and loved her for it, and wanted to comfort her. And . . . she was right. I knew that, too. It was a shame I returned more and more to my mother's way of thinking once that ebullient trophy moment passed into history.

I was, for a time, attracted to opiates, almost as if I'd internalized James and his craving during the 1970s. My favorites for almost a year were Percocets combined with Quaaludes (half of one, half of the other), which seemed to make me happy, or at least not unhappy. After six months, I began to start spinning and rotating, and they made me dull and lugubrious momentarily, and then once again ashamed. I was drawn toward that flash of a light-filled moment that the character Brick, in *Cat on a Hot Tin Roof*, refers to as the "click"—those ten seconds when something in your conscious mind and body opens its doors to the slow quixotic flood of the hypnagogic state, shutting down all fears, twitches, paranoias, and shaky needs for control.

But a critical component and attraction of my love of pills was privacy, secrecy, no one knowing or ever suspecting a thing. Relishing the aloneness of it all, the danger, the adrenaline. That urge to be bad. The urge to seem like I was there, even though I wasn't. The battle of opposites, self-destruction in a tug-of-war against the life-surge of self-protection. Yes, I was emulating James in some big, perverse way, but maybe I would have done the same thing without James as a model. The most curious question, and one that still remains, is what was it that lightened my heart and my mind, made me positive and gregarious?

Was it the Prozac or the Oscar?

THAT YEAR, 1989, was a good one for me, though less good, at least in a material way, for my husband. Throughout the late eighties and early nineties, I found myself praying for "some kind of success-in-the-world for Jim." However, while he received a few letters from publishing people that were complimentary, most stopped a few inches short of jubilant acceptance.

Whether it had to do with the fate of his book, or Jim not working a real job, or the general state of our marriage, our homes in New York and the Vineyard continued to teem with our silent noons and angry dawns. I asked myself, How could anyone hold his own sharing the drenched tutu that was my life?

He just doesn't get it, I would think. My love is eroding swiftly, and nothing is changing. Maybe it's eroding *because* nothing is changing. Then, the usual hasty reversal of feelings: Jim and I are both too special to be bringing out the worst in each other. At one point, Jim, who had begun leasing a separate writing and living studio on West Ninety-seventh Street, relocated his office to the tower of our Central Park West apartment, which I had rented from the landlords way back when James and I shared the apartment. It was reachable only by a spooky changing of elevators. I couldn't help but recall James's self-exile to that exact same tower—wordless and blank, like the third ghost in *A Christmas Carol*. Did I do something to make them want or need to remove themselves? And what did their private lives really entail?

Mixed with my exasperation was my paranoia that Jim was cheating on me. That he'd fallen in love with another woman who, in my imagination, was easier to live with and more deserving of all the things he *did* have to offer. Someone who didn't put all this ungodly material pressure on him. My suspicions worsened when Jim began attending a writing workshop at the Sixty-third Street YMCA, where I assumed—because my brain worked that way—that all the other students (female) had fallen in love with him.

· · ·

I'VE ALWAYS HAD a spy living in my own head, which is maybe why, when I decided to hire a real private eye, I was simply rounding things out! Snake—yes, that was really his name—lived in New Jersey, and a trustworthy friend had given me his contact information. First, though, I called Jackie to tell her about my plan. I was initially hesitant. Not wanting to give it all away, asking myself, "Oh, come on, Carly, what exactly is there to give away?"

Jackie told me to be careful, and even offered her own private detective if I wanted to make his acquaintance.

"But Snake sounds so—" What were the words I was looking for? "So . . . *impressively unreliable*—so unreal, so like a cartoon of whoever he is! Which is what I think I'm going to want, Jackie. I don't *want* to believe anything bad or conclusive about Jim, I want to overrule it!"

I called my detective. Snake had a New York/Bronx/Brooklyn accent with overtones of somewhere in the hinterlands of Hoodlum City. He asked for five thousand up front, gas in the car, good faith, trench coat (I wished). I sent him ten pictures of Jim. Every angle of his face and his statuesque tall strong body. I never laid eyes on Snake, so this is a pretty fair description of one of our exchanges:

SNAKE: *Well, I see him now. He's on Fifty-seventh, coming out of a store called Bendel? Yeah, Bendel. Like meddle or maybe kettle. He's got a shopping bag . . . yeah, I think it's a book bag. Maybe a brown paper bag or somethin'.*

ME: *Stay with him!* (My astute instructions came from my lifetime of experience with TV crime shows.)

SNAKE: *He's makin' a turn on Fifty-ninth Street, on Central Park South. Oh, oh, wait! He's going in a little store with antique kind of like things. Yeah.* (Heavy breathing.) *Yeah, he's still in there, looks like he's making some kind of deal. He's talkin' to the proprietor. You know what I mean? Okay. Here he comes. He's empty-handed.*

I heard an obvious puff on his cigarette, a long inhale and undisguised, equally long exhale.

ME: *You mean he's left the shopping bag he had coming out of Bendel's?*

SNAKE: *No—he's got that. He's walking fast and seems he is getting into a cab. Yup. That's it—a cab.*

ME: *Follow him!*

SNAKE: *Okay, they're headed west across Central Park South, and now he's just going down Seventh Ave. There they go. Bingo. There's not too much traffic, they're speeding. Oh, God. Speeding.*

ME: *Speeding? You mean he's trying to lose you?* (I hear strains of a female singer.)

SNAKE: *Well, let's see . . .* (I start to hear Lena Horne singing over his radio.)

ME: *Snake, could you please turn your radio lower? I can't hear you.*

SNAKE: *Sorry about that. Better? Okay, we are looking at some new decision by the cabdriver and the target. Looks like they are headed uptown. I'll try and follow. Yup. I still have a yarn on them. A lead. Yup. I got 'em. They're fighting the Christmas traffic on Amsterdam. Wait, a bus is in the way. Oh, jeez.*

ME: *Stay with him. He's probably going to his apartment on Ninety-seventh Street and Broadway.*

SNAKE: *That's where the two of yez live?*

ME: *Complicated. No. Just he lives there. He writes there. Where are they now?*

SNAKE: *Wait! They're going west. Looks like the West Side Highway. Yip. They're going to the West Side Highway. Bingo!*

ME: *The bridge? They're going to the entrance to the bridge?*

SNAKE: *No, but the George Washington Bridge is probably next. Speedin' up the West. That's them all right. Bingo!*

ME (thinking): He has an office in New Jersey forty-five minutes up the Palisades, but why is he going there on a Wednesday night with a present from Bendel's for a woman? My head is swimming with facts, names, times. God damn him. He's due home in an hour. (Soon there would be cell phones, but I didn't have one until 1991.)

SNAKE: *Okay, now we're getting somewhere. I got 'em getting off at the 178th Street entrance to the bridge.*

ME: *Good going, Snake!* (I can't believe I'm saying that name.) *Keep going. Good going.*

Snake is a little quiet for the next ten seconds.

SNAKE: *Hold on. Jeez, he got on the lower level.*

ME: *Yes??*

SNAKE: *I think I must be on the upper level. I can't find him. Oh, I guess I lost 'em.*

ME: *You lost him? How? Shit!*

SNAKE: *You said it: shit is it! What do you want me to do now?*

I let Snake keep the down payment. For the time being, my angst over Jim and his sly remove went underground. We spent a nice Christmas together, and although there were a few times when I thought I maybe should have taken Jackie up on her security guard, I decided just to allow a lot of hairy nuggets of dust to exist under the rug until I had some definite knowledge.

Was it the tension and even the bizarreness in Jim's and my marriage in the early nineties that inspired Jackie to invite me to build a small cabin on her property in Aquinnah? I believed she meant it, too, at least in the moment. Assuming she was just being charming, I let the subject drop, only for Jackie to bring up the idea again a week later, adding that I could stay at Caroline's and John's quarters as my prospective cabin was being built. I had never had such a loving invitation. "An artist's cabin," she embellished on her fantasy.

I just adore her so much, I wrote in my diary, *and that worship must be gently patted down and kept at bay.*

Fortunately or not, I was distracted from the vicissitudes of my marriage by the social goings-on of the Vineyard in August. I wrote in my diary:

> *A party on Saturday at my house with too many heavy-hitters left me prey to my body and head doing loop-de-loops . . . At the tea party, along with everybody's*

children, were Jackie and her dear friend Maurice Tempelsman, Kay Graham, Steven Spielberg and Kate Capshaw, George Lucas, Kathleen Kennedy and Frank Marshall; in fact, my mother was there too and most pleased to be so—oh God, it was awful!

How could I say something self-effacing about a really nice party? Someone quickly explain this to me!

I'm bloated with too much social interaction and Vineyard August-ness, and just so tired, and my diary entry trails off, depleted.

Tops in the ongoing summertime social excitement was the party Jim and I went to at the renowned publisher Katharine Graham's house to welcome President and First Lady Bill and Hillary Clinton on their first visit to the Vineyard. I remember giving Jackie a moment-by-moment account of the party, and the Clintons' visit to my house the very next day. The two of us sat in my circle garden amid the late summer marigolds and sunflowers, drinking white wine spritzers and eating cucumber sandwiches. It was so humid and the ice was melting so fast in our glasses that it made a crinkly, collapsing sound that, to my mind at least, ice has no business making.

The morning of the party, Jackie had gone sailing with the Clintons on the *Relamar*, the yacht belonging to her close companion, the businessman and diamond merchant Maurice Tempelsman, though she declined the party itself, preferring to skip out on the official welcome.

"You would have laughed and laughed, and then it would have been all over," I said, referring to the dinner at Kay's.

"Who was sitting where?" Jackie asked.

I told Jackie that for whatever reason, I was placed at the "A" table, Kay's table. She sat at the head like a much grimmer, more knuckle-rapping version of Miss Jean Brodie. There were three other large round tables in the formal dining room, along with place cards like exam grades. (Jackie, I knew, was also a place-card user, whereas I had never in my life given that kind of dinner party.)

I couldn't really remember the cocktail portion of the night, I told her, "but I do remember every detail of the *dinner*, since it was so traumatic." Jackie's face was eager and intense, waiting to be unfurled by the gossip my expression seemed to promise. She was obviously relieved not to have been there. "Who was sitting where?" she repeated, ready to gain a mental picture of the tableau.

"Kay was at the head table. President Clinton was sitting on her right," I went on, "with [former secretary of state] Henry Kissinger on her left. On the other side of Clinton was [former *Vogue* editor] Louise Grunwald, then [former attorney general] Nicholas Katzenbach, then Lally Weymouth, Kay's daughter, followed by Lawrence Eagleburger [yet *another* former secretary of state], then me.

"Why do I think [former secretary of defense] Robert McNamara was there? *Would* he have been there?" I asked Jackie.

"Well, he's a great friend of Kay's."

"Yes—in fact, Kay asked me to sing to him last summer over the phone. She wanted me to take him away from his wife, in fact . . . so *she* could marry him!"

"Oh, Carly, you didn't follow through, did you?"

Chuckling, I couldn't resist: "Jackie, I'm surprised you didn't know that I've been pimping for Kay for years."

Kay had recently revealed to me that her first choice in a husband was Warren Buffett. She didn't get Buffett (I guess I wasn't very successful as a pimp) and she would next set her sights on McNamara. Her third choice was Mike.

"Doesn't it seem like Mike is on everybody's list?" Jackie commented rhetorically. Then she asked me what I wore.

"Oh, my lord, I think I looked a little trampy. I wore a bustier"—bustiers were in fashion at the time, as Madonna had made them mainstream—"and very long earrings, to make me look less naked. Bill was looking at me very flatteringly. I don't know if I was just imagining it. I wore my hair up, too, which I don't usually do, with wisps coming and going and getting caught in the earrings. If I do say so myself, I looked fetching, and I was blushing, too, like Scarlett, or was it perimenopause?"

"What about the conversations?"

"Well, *that* was actually the disaster," I said, adding that Jim was seated at Hillary's table, and therefore wasn't there to save me from any political mishaps. Neither did Kay take any great pains to hide a sheath of index cards on which she'd written germane questions to ask all the assembled past and present great political luminaries, crowned by the president. "The subject of the night was *NAFTA*! Yes, I knew the acronym, NAFTA, but its meaning [North American Free Trade Agreement] was just out of reach. I had absolutely no idea what to say if the inevitable question came around to me: *What did I think of NAFTA?*"

I explained how Kay was very formal, as always, and she went around the table in order of seating. When it was close to being my turn, I thought about going to the bathroom, my old trick from school that I called on whenever I was afraid to answer a question and thereby exhibit my stammer to the classmates. But lo and behold, what to my wandering eyes should appear but a late arrival. Webb Hubbell, the Arkansas lawyer and writer. Most important, Bill Clinton's close friend.

"Oh, no, what a *relief*."

"Anyhow, as soon as Webb arrived, I was home safe," I told Jackie. "He and I were both terrified by how formal everything was, and we turned toward each other and started making small talk. 'What was Little Rock like at Christmas?' 'How long have you lived there?' 'How long have you, Carly, lived here?' 'Where is your husband?' 'What does he do?'"

"*CAWWLY*," boomed the voice of an evil stepmother, "*BRING IT BACK TO THE CENTER!*"

I looked up at the person who had broadcast the command: Kay, her hands and fingers stretched out like lobster claws. Her face was unspeakably fierce. But it was also the *way* she'd said my name. A lot of sphincter pressure was placed on the first syllable as she bore down on the *AW*-syllable. It wasn't a friendly, rounded *R*, but a *CAW-LEE*, the sound of a large crow being beaten to death with a bat.

"How embarrassing. How awful. What was she doing that for? Why didn't she blurt out the same thing to Webb Hubbell?"

"I suppose Webb was spared because he was a friend of Bill's."

Amid my extreme self-consciousness and embarrassment, I was also praying this wasn't presaging the inevitable question about NAFTA that I was dreading. "What was NAFTA? NAFTA, let's see. It was a *treaty*! Was it anything like perestroika? Or maybe *détente*? Oh, Jackie, I know *nothing*. I forgot *everything*!"

"You don't—don't be silly. You just weed out the boring things."

"Then—thank God—after I faced the table as Kay commanded, Beverly Sills [the opera singer] arrived for dessert. She sat down between Webb and me. I launched into a feverish discussion with her about my opera singer sister, Joey, with whom Beverly was great friends. If only I'd been sitting next to Jim, he would have saved me. Or Rose [Styron]. Where in the world was Rose?"

"When she's not everywhere, where is she?"

"So I was deep in that close, face-to-face discussion with Beverly, who did not know the Kay rule that everyone's face had to be pointed to the center." Then the stern, fearsome, malevolent voice of the wicked stepmother called out for a second time, guillotining all conversation:

"*CAWLY... BRING IT BACK TO THE CENTER!*"

"Jackie, I was completely *mortified*. I looked at the president, and he was looking at me as though he realized and understood I was being systematically tortured. Which made me start tearing up. I teared up and up and up, until a few tears made little paths down my cheeks. I think Bill was about to say something and, in fact, did. He changed the subject completely to something about the Vineyard."

I was aware that Jackie was loving this story as much as I was horrified telling it. It was obvious she knew every person I was talking about, and no doubt had her own "reveal" about them, which she might have kept to herself only because I was putting so much energy into my own story. More likely, she was being discreet.

"If nothing else did, it was his sheer empathy that made the relationship between the president and me so immediate. He really was appalled, and he told me that later.

"After dinner," I continued, "all the guests repaired to Kay's white living room for coffee and dessert. It was there that, after treating me like a truant kindergartner, Kay had the audacity to ask me to *sing*. I don't mean to do Kay any disservice," I said, "but truly, it didn't look good. I mean for *her*.

"Ignoring my sour attitude, she asked me to sing 'My Funny Valentine.' She'd hired another musician I know slightly, named Jeremy Berlin, to play cocktail music, and if I'd known she was planning to ask me to sing, Jeremy and I could have rehearsed, or at least prepared *something*. Instead, Jeremy sat at a small electric piano, like Schroeder in *Peanuts*, and I began singing . . . well, whatever the first note was that came to me. I certainly don't have perfect pitch, and I didn't mean for Jeremy to follow me, but it was too late, the note had already hit the air. It was obvious to both of us I'd chosen an unplayable key. Poor Jeremy! As he poked around for the notes, I kept trying to help him by changing my note to match *his*. My funny valentine-valentine-valentine, up and up, trying to land on the right note."

"Oh, no! And were people sitting or standing or singing along?"

"All three. As Jeremy and I searched for a landing place, some people took seats. There were white couches everywhere. You know what Kay's living room is like. It makes you . . ."

". . . have the urge to spill a nice big glass of red wine?" Jackie had finished my thought for me, and as we poured more wine into our glasses, we giggled.

"Was John Kerry there?" Jackie asked.

"I think he was *not*. But I don't know. There must have been forty people there!"

"I like John a lot," Jackie said. "You know he has the same initials as Jack."

Jackie's laugh made it sound less than serious, though it didn't seem an unlikely match, either. She and John Kerry shared a similar patrician tallness—an unswerving head atop a long neck. John Kerry and JFK were alike, too, in other ways. They'd learned their manners from similar prep schools in the Northeast, and they'd gone straight into Massachusetts politics. And they have the same initials.

"Did you ever . . . 'take a walk'?" I said, using Edna O'Brien's strange and lovely euphemism, feeling as though it was permitted because it was obscure, and also it was beginning to rain and I felt heady from the wine. She changed the subject with charm and a practiced alacrity and we resumed talking about "My Funny Valentine," how it finally found its key and how even Kissinger sang *vit hiss Cherman accent oll srue de song.*

"Afterward I was completely giddy with laughter, and Bill sat with his arm around Hillary, and once it was over, the illustrious—and yes, I do mean illustrious—gathered around. How did you ever get used to it, Jackie?"

"It all gets just like the cast of *The Howdy Doody Show* after a while," she said. "You know, you forget you're sitting next to the person who signed some treaty you're supposed to know the ins and outs of . . . and then 'Oh, look,' you say, 'there's that very famous, familiar man,' and you should remember his name, and well, you remember all of a sudden that . . . it's just Teddy! Except he's wearing a tuxedo! Your mind just flips back to when you helped him with his math homework. It seems so close. It *is* so close. It's absurd, isn't it?"

By now the rain was picking up and I asked Jackie if she felt like going inside, though before I did that, I took a long look at her. She looked so beautiful and translucent in her white peasant blouse, her hair swept back in a bun at the nape of her neck. I'm not at all nervous with her now, I thought. This is the best I've ever felt with her. It might have had something to do with the surrounding flowers, especially the wayward cosmos and overgrown mint, and how the rain seemed to merge the scents and beauty of the garden, and of her, as one.

But she wanted to know even more. "What else did you sing at Kay's? Did anyone else sing?"

I told her that the best was yet to come. "Hillary said, 'Do you know any Everly Brothers songs?' And, of course, who doesn't, so Bill chimed in and requested 'Dream.' That one was easy to find the key for, and everyone in the room, all those secretaries of state, Walter Cronkite and Susie Trees, and Beverly Sills, and the Grunwalds, and Mike and Mary Wallace, Bill and Rose, and even Jim joined in and sang most beautifully."

When I want you in my arms, when I want you and all your charms, whenever I want you, all I have to do is dream, dream, dream, dream . . .

That wasn't the end, though, I noted. When "Dream" was over, someone called out, "What about 'Sittin' on the Dock of the Bay'?" "Bill began singing it," I said, "while Hillary tapped her thighs, and somehow the electric piano found the right notes. I sang harmonies, but Kay thought I was singing the melody, and tried to follow me. After it was over, or at least we thought it was over, Henry Kissinger—I mean, Jackie, you can't imagine how truly, amazingly, dauntingly funny it was—started a brand-new verse. It was something about 'Sittin' on the morning swing, I'll be sittin' when the evening rings . . .' and everyone just let him go on by himself, and once it was over the whole room burst into applause and laughter. I think it was the high point of the musical history of the Vineyard."

"In retrospect," Jackie said, "I wish I had decided to come."

THE DAY AFTER the memorable night at Kay's, the First Family came to my house for lunch. It was planned at the very last minute, and the amount of preparation was slim. The rules were just us, meaning my immediate family: Jim, Sally, and Ben. No one else.

What I remember most vividly was the presence on my property of a team of Secret Service men and women. Some were nestling in trees with instruments to survey the grounds, and others ventured inside the house to check all the closets and other places where they just might stumble across enemy soldiers still in hiding from the Korean War.

There were also "tasters"—the intrepid personnel tasked with sampling the soup and the quiche, the carrots and the corn, the breads and the pies, before they touched the lips of the First Family. It was one of the tasters, in fact, who told me the chicken soup I'd made just that morning tasted "funny." Well, yes, because I'd been expecting the Clintons for lunch, but their arrival kept getting delayed by round after round of golf, so by 5 p.m., when the taster brought the spoon to his mouth, the soup was contaminated by overcooking and 98 percent humidity, and yes, it did taste "funny," which was a polite way of saying "inedible." Assuring the taster that I was not involved in a sinister plot, that it was simply a matter of timing, and of me, the cook, not paying sufficient attention, down the kitchen disposal it went. I quickly phoned a local friend, a professional chef, who said she could put together a quiche and a salad with goat cheese within the hour.

During this whole time, as I was getting more and more concerned as to where the Clintons could possibly be, I kept in constant phone contact with Jackie, who kindly put up with my hair-pulling and growing tension, saying finally, as only Jacqueline Kennedy Onassis could or would, *"Oh, Carly, for Christ's sake, it's just another president!"*

The Clintons and their daughter, Chelsea (then eleven years old), arrived at around 6 p.m., which coincided with seventeen-year-old Sally and fourteen-year-old Ben's arrival off the plane from China, where they'd vacationed with James. My caretakers, Jimmy LeRoux and his wife, Wendy, were there to help me coordinate everyone's comings and goings. They also treated one of the tree-spy Secret Service men for a nasty wasp sting he'd gotten as he scrambled down out of a nearby white birch. The Clintons, Jim, Sally, Ben, and I all sat at my small round dining room table. Bill and Hillary were both dressed in short-sleeve sport shirts, and Hillary wore plaid Bermuda shorts, while Chelsea flatteringly imitated the way Sally had her hair up in a knot, crisscrossed with a chopstick to hold it in place. Bill and Hillary took turns describing the day they first saw each other in the Yale Law School library. The story still seemed thrilling to them, despite how many times they must have told it.

Day turned into night, and after a lengthy tour of my house, we swung on the outdoor swings and felt a friendship I hoped we would preserve. The line of black cars pulled out of the drive at 9 p.m., and we, the Simon-Taylor-Harts, sat down to relive the day's highlights, including the moment Bill Clinton condemned in no uncertain terms how unfairly he thought Kay Graham had treated me. He whispered in my ear: "She sure did give you a hard time."

All that night, Bill looked at me with the same keen, kinetic energy he'd displayed at Kay's party. Which one of us had entered the other's magnetic field is questionable, but the combination of "it's nothing personal" and "it's exceptionally personal" made me consider the misunderstandings he would experience later on in a different light. He never lost the heady aroma of his visceral being.

Bill Clinton has "the Glint," I told Jackie afterward—the Glint being a subtle knowingness, a certainty of your effect on others, the assurance that just maybe you know more about them than they know about themselves. It all comes through the eyes. "At Kay's, I couldn't look directly into his eyes for more than a second. I noticed that unmistakable grasp of my energy meeting up with his."

"The Glint," she said. "I just love that as a description."

I know everything there is to know about the Glint, I told her. "I have it, too! So I always recognize the feeling when I'm doing it, or when I'm being 'done to.'" The first time I remembered having the Glint was back in sixth grade. I was sitting in a classroom, eight rows in, and staring at the shoulder blades of a boy named Kenny who was seated in the first row. The Glint I aimed at his back made him turn around, and when he did, our eyes meshed. My energy practically *forced* him to look back at me. Or so I told myself. Was I deluded? Was it some party trick? It wasn't like I had a crush on Kenny, not like the one I had on another boy who sat on the other side of the room. I had no idea what I was doing when I sent out the Glint, or what its ultimate purpose might have been. "When I did that to Kenny, I *owned* him," I told Jackie. "Seriously! I'm not making it up! The Glint isn't necessarily sexual—but it's not *unsexual*, either. The Glint has something more to do with some crazy, charismatic, weirdly adrenalized power."

Jackie was curious about this "little act of courage," as she called it. "Did someone teach you? Did you learn it from someone? Imitate it?"

"I think I must have unconsciously learned the Glint from Clark Gable as Rhett Butler in *Gone with the Wind*. Remember what he did to Scarlett? But *only* to Scarlett?"

We talked about various other people who we thought had the Glint. We agreed that one of the conditions of having the Glint is that you *know* you have it. Marlon Brando had the Glint, especially when he makes his first appearance in his sweat-soaked T-shirt in the film version of *A Streetcar Named Desire*. As he prowls the cramped room with Blanche DuBois looking on, I remember feeling a waviness, a suspension of gravity, in the pit of my stomach, one that correlated with the same feeling somewhere in the center of my forehead. I wanted to laugh. Not because Brando was funny, because he wasn't. He was in charge, and his physical confidence made my whole being lift up like a balloon. I felt an airy mirth, just as I had when I was hypnotized once for smoking.

Like Rhett Butler and Marlon Brando, Bill Clinton seemed to know the same trick. His eyes could entice women into a dangerous neighborhood. Bill would get into trouble. Jackie and I agreed that our new president most definitely had the Glint.

Back the way it was before

Before the door was opened

Back the way it was before

Before the ice was broken

Back the way it used to be

Everyone thought I was funny

But nobody ever asked me

If I wanted tiny little sandwiches

Sent up to my room

—"BACK THE WAY"

7

The Show Must Go On

I T WAS EARLY WINTER 1991, and I was past holiday parties and in the midst of recording a score for Nora Ephron's directorial film debut, *This Is My Life*, based on Meg Wolitzer's novel, about a female comedian and her fraught relationship with her two young daughters. One of the songs, "Love of My Life," which I had written for and about Ben and Sally, fit the movie perfectly. I shot a video, starring teenage Ben, who played guitar and moved gracefully around the set, and in general played a mildly

Oedipal version of himself, while I gazed at him with very real love.

Jim and I were getting along, at least until one thing or another interrupted our daily meanderings in the confused forest of our marriage. The interruption this time centered around a poem that I found on top of Jim's bedroom bureau. Jim had been writing more and more exquisite poems over the past few years, and in many of them I was able to recognize myself as the heroine. But in this poem, the protagonist was described as having a full head of black hair. The poem's subject was an apparently new young love walking, with a dancer's grace, past a church into a Greenwich Village subway station. Well, immediate panic sent me straight inside the tangled chaos of my sewing basket. Slipping my thumb and index finger into a nifty little pair of sewing shears, I grabbed Jim's clothes off the bureau, plus a few others I pulled from the drawers—a hat, boxer shorts, a necktie—scissoring away like a mad seamstress, while also frisking them like a policewoman for whatever items might be secreted in the pockets.

I took a closer look at the poem. The words "your dark furry beard" jumped out at me. I had a gut reaction. My heart started beating outside of my chest. I stabbed the scissors into the wall of our bedroom—our womb, our wigwam, the center of Jim's and my togetherness. With the wall-stabbing over, I closed down. I shut myself off. I would deal with everything later. What's the worst that it could be, anyway? The bearded lady in the circus? I was confused and overcome. But, stalwart, I reminded myself that, thankfully, I had a lot to do. I had to get ready for Jackie and Alec Baldwin, and my recently exposed husband Jim, who was late coming home with the Pouilly-Fuissé and the chocolate cake I'd asked him to buy—all ingredients for the evening ahead, which would involve half a dozen Irish spinster sisters, and a bit of subterfuge.

A few weeks earlier, Jackie had mentioned "what fun" it would be to go see *Dancing at Lughnasa*, Brian Friel's play about a family of unmarried middle-aged sisters living together in a cottage on the west coast of Ireland. At the time, Maurice was off somewhere, likely making an impressive purchase of diamond mines. With Maurice out of town, I proposed a casual "double date" consisting of Jim, me, Jackie, and a fourth person yet to be determined. Jackie responded with another schoolgirl-like utterance of excitement, which I have to think was based on her belief, erroneous or not, that I knew a lot of extremely interesting people.

In the past, Jackie and I had talked about Ken Burns, who was not only a close friend of mine, but someone I had recently worked with on his PBS series *Baseball*. I got in touch with Ken, but he was out of town, filming yet another epic PBS series. Ken asked for—no, strongly requested—a rain check. I suggested Joe Armstrong, Jackie's close friend. She said, "Absolutely." But Joe was in Texas. That's when Jim suggested Alec Baldwin, a buddy of his.

"We'll have to go *undercover*."

"What about wigs? I can be Jean Harlow!" Jackie exclaimed. She was fully in the moment and also looking forward not only to another routine escapade but also to an evening that might well require advanced levels of dexterous espionage!

"I've got wigs!" By now I was outside of myself, feeling as excited as a dog when his food is coming in a few seconds, his tail gone wild on serotonin.

"Yes—" And Jackie brought up the video for my song "Tired of Being Blonde," which was directed by Jeremy Irons, who had been a guest in my house with his wife, Sinéad Cusack, and their little boy Sam—one of those families that are English, yes, but American enough to put their drinks on the table. "You must have all kinds!" Jackie said, meaning wigs—not English actors.

"Oh, yes," I told her. I had red wigs, pixie-cut wigs, purple wigs, and even wigs designed to be worn by Madame de Pompadour. Our excited chatter rose like an overture of big, deep, swelling Jackie-laughter, especially when she told me how much she would love to see Alec Baldwin in a Madame de Pompadour wig. "Oh, *do* get Jim to ask Alec."

Jim was good to his word, and Alec, who had never met Jackie, was in a state of hyper-disbelief. "Jackie Kennedy wants to go on a *date* with *me*?" he said. "Are you *kidding*?" Alec's incredulity gradually gave way to "What should I wear?" followed by "Uh—*what* was the name of the play you say we are going to?"

Despite the devastating poem I'd found on Jim's dresser, I acted as though nothing was wrong, the evening ahead blotting out the shock of my own reality distortion. I would think about it later, tomorrow, next week, never. I wasn't about to ruin everybody's evening with my worried little face. The show must go on!

THAT NIGHT, Jackie, Alec, Jim, and I sat around my small pine wine-tasting French provincial table, eating chicken I'd prepared with dark syrup cherries and hollandaise sauce. As anticipated, Jackie doted on Alec, and Alec, despite his been-there, seen-everything show business poise, occasionally revealed the lightest possible slick of sweat on his brow. Dressed in a black-and-white cashmere Armani sweater, her businesswoman's gold Cartier watch flashing like a possible UFO, Jackie was ravishing, her rapt, wide-eyed "just for you" expression seeming to shut out everyone in the room but Alec. Did I recognize the Glint?

Jackie seemed at peace that night, inspired by what I'd always imagined to be a lifelong sense of mischief, borne during her debutante days, carried through numerous horseback rides and jumps, maintained through decades of flashbulbs and photographs, and grief, and relief, then relived grief. No doubt that mischief had carried her places she never imagined she would go. It had helped cushion her from the haunting and the horror of post-traumatic stress disorder, a condition she feared might never leave her alone. But that night she was in deliriously good form, a mischief-lover and mischief-maker delighting in the altogether ridic-ulous prank the four of us had up our sleeves, or rather, atop our pates.

When the meal was over, but before the chocolate cake was served, I went into my bedroom, stepping over the rib-bony casualties of Jim's cut-up boxer shorts. Had Jim been in our room to see the damage yet? If so, it would have been hard for him, or anybody, to put two and two together. Determined, I brought out my suitcase of wigs. There must have been half a dozen of them in all—one for each of us, and two extras, if the mood struck.

Jim, brave-faced and laughing, was the first to put his on, a long, curly Eddie Van Halen wig that prompted a cho-rus of laughter. Alec chose a short, brown one; mine was comely, blond, and Grand Ole Opry–esque, and Jackie reached impulsively for the one befitting Madame de Pom-padour. Our shrieks of laughter made us sound like chick-ens being chased around a barnyard. Jackie's wig became her, a sign of her lineage, the sides of her own brown hair setting off two new gray Gallic sideburns.

When the downstairs buzzer rang to summon us, I didn't bother to glance in the hallway mirror. I'd ordered us a car, but Jackie, no slouch, had arranged for her own car and driver to pick her up. With her Pompadour wig on her head, she whispered that she would meet us at the theater, before racing out the door onto the elevator. It wasn't rude; it was, as usual, cagey.

With our wigs firmly in place, Jim, Alec, and I found our own waiting car, though before we all climbed into the back seat, I took a small slug of vodka. Unfortunately, a photographer from the *New York Post* was hiding outside my apartment building, and a photo of me wearing my wig, tippling my flask, appeared in the paper early the next morning. Not the best photo, but what was there to lose? Jackie, the photographer's real prize, had done some last-minute trick with mirrors and slid like air into the back seat of her fog-shrouded limousine. And as she drove off, she took with her our reason for wearing wigs in the first place and left all of us looking like fools as we exited the building.

Pulling up to the theater, we all decided to leave our wigs behind in the car. They lay there on the back seat, dejected, like puppies disappointed there would be no walks that day. There was no fanfare except for our own secret, slightly whimsical smiles, and my overriding worry was that I had all four tickets with me, so where was Jackie, and, more important, would she still be wearing her Madame de Pompadour ringlets?

The answer was "already seated." When we found her, Jackie was alone in the fourth row, with three empty seats separating her from the aisle. She probably left Madame de Pompadour in the car, and undoubtedly reassured the ticket taker with her famous smile. Should I sit next to her? Should

Alec? In the end, she and I sat together, and soon the room grew dark and the audience did, too.

First thing next morning, Jackie called to tell me what a magical evening it was, how divine Alec was, and how important she felt it was to think and act and cavort like a child now and again. She also said she could now understand why I loved Jim so much. "He's such fun and so smart." In general, Jackie alternated between calling me on the phone and writing me the most beautiful, charming, funny little notes on her well-known light blue stationery, her name inscribed in small black block letters across the top. In a bound book I still keep all the correspondence I received from Jackie over the years. Her words and handwriting were always gracious, elegant, swooping, romantic, and quietly very funny.

When *Amy the Dancing Bear* came out, Jackie called me up after a successful book signing.

"Carly, can you believe it? All those people lining up for you to tell them bedtime stories!"

Another time she sent me a black beanbag eye-band to help me with my insomnia, with a short note about wishing me a rapturous doze.

ON AND OFF my whole life, sleep had been a casualty of my anxiety. It so happened that my experiment with Prozac lasted more or less for a few years—but as is true of most of life, it didn't save me, either. What was I looking for? As always, a bit too much. By spring of 1992, I was using pills to fill in a whole series of bad blanks. The thing about depressive thinking is that as another person is talking, you're busy projecting hundreds of demeaning small hells into their pauses, stammers, blinks, and throat-clearings, and even when you know exactly what you're doing, it doesn't matter. If life were a movie, the director would step in, cutting away to a white oak bending in the wind, or a Labrador retriever rooting its nose under the bedcovers. But outside of the movies, the human brain needs to be completely occupied.

By March of that year, I was trying, desperately and in vain, to stay away from the undertow, and talking to Jackie about the pros and cons of medicating oneself. She knew full well how anxious I was, knew I had to take Valium, and seemed to accept this state of affairs completely. I couldn't explain how exactly, but pills were a subject familiar to her, a dance that either she'd danced herself or seen others dancing. Still, she was never someone who pried. She uncharacteristically asked me if my pill use was "a problem." "No," I remember telling her, "it's an *answer!*" As she and I walked up Madison Avenue one day, past window after window of alien-like mannequins attired in violently overpriced clothes, Jackie told me that LSD was used fairly routinely in the 1950s.

"Clare Boothe Luce used to have parties where guests were split up into different groups: the ones *in* the bedroom, and the ones *pretending* to be in the living room." We both laughed, and I got the meaning, even though it was attractively obscure.

"Were you ever interested in trying hallucinogenics?" I

asked, not wanting to overstep any boundaries but doing it anyway.

"You know, it was the kind of thing you really didn't talk about then. There seemed to be a restraint that came with Eisenhower. I don't know just who pulled the plug on their legality. Let's see if I can remember the last party where it was, you know, *fun*, and not too serious . . ."

As we continued up Madison, I wanted to ask Jackie about Dr. Max Jacobson, known as "Miracle Max" and "Dr. Feelgood," who was famous in the fifties and sixties for giving his celebrity clientele, including JFK, amphetamines, steroids, painkillers, and other merry cocktails before the feds revoked his medical license in the mid-1970s. Enough had been written about how Dr. Jacobson provided relief for poor Jack's back, and how Jackie also needed to keep up "her endurance and her stride." But I never heard it directly from her. She never let her guard down in that way, or gave even one explicit hint, except once during a party at her house, when a friend of mine had hurt his back and Jackie offered him a few pellets: "These are the ones Jack used to take for HIS back." I wondered if they actually came from an old black leather case that the president left behind or they were just "similar" pills.

THAT PARTICULAR MARCH, I may have been less subtle in the amount of subduing I was doing to quiet my noise. Jim and his "program friends" decided I was worthy of a twenty-eight-day trip to a local rehab called the Summer House. It was the discovery of one of my pellet stews that drew it to Jim's attention. I went along with it. The Summer House attracted both street types and wealthy addicts, with some emphasis on the former. The staff members, while perhaps well-intentioned, were dreary.

What a crazy thing to say. Some were there because they really wanted to help others. I now see it as a way Jim could live his life without scrutiny: "Get Carly a little healthy holiday behind locked windows and doors." I imagined there were many winks out of sight. That's not really true, but when I was leaving home with my little suitcase, I wasn't thinking kindly about those who dictated my course.

Upon checking in, the first thing I had to do was to turn in my "sharps." Very dangerous to have any tweezers, obviously, but had I known, I would have made sure I had my legs waxed before leaving home. Detoxing and stubbly at the same time would never be my choice. I was allowed one call a day. They all ended up being to Jackie, with the exception of one to my extended family, who were not nearly as interested as she was. I needed levity. Not that it was all that funny by any means. Group meetings did not get off to a good start:

"You better take a good look at yourself, Miss Uptight Uptown."

The stories from the group, 98 percent men, were harrowing. No wonder I was "Uptight Uptown." Some of them had been in prison for years. A few of them had killed family members for money to procure drugs. Still, feeling no symptoms of withdrawal, I was asked by my counselor on the third day to write a story where I was talking to my pills as if they were human beings: "Oh, hello, Hank, you handsome old thing . . . I sure could use your comfort just about now."

The group understood that I was trying to make light of it and made me start the story over for the next session. That night, I slipped into the smoking room, where there were five men (and boys) of different colors and stripes.

"So what's a song I might know of yours?" a man named Roger asked me slightly aggressively.

"I don't think you'd know one, but I heard *you* singing one of my favorite songs as I came up behind the door."

"Oh, yeah, that was 'Lean on Me.'"

"Can I sing with you?" The air was redolent with smoke so thick that it could put you in a real hospital.

The room went silent until I poked my voice into the haze: "Lean on me when you're not strong, I'll be your friend, I'll help you carry on . . ."

As one voice was overlaid on another, the tone and thrust got punchier. I sang harmony, and there was one very skinny older gent in overalls who was singing an octave lower than anyone else and skillfully wove in and out bass notes with an original jazz phrasing. As if he was a stand-up bass player, he moved his finger up and down imaginary frets, accenting with his head, leading with the chin. What a present. I asked him to please sing louder, as he was very humble and didn't want to show off and maybe didn't want to hear himself. I, on the other hand, was singing out more than I ever had. It was comforting in the most bizarre way. No threats anywhere. Except the smoke. I'd deal with that if I stayed. Only I wasn't planning to stay.

I told Jackie that night that I hadn't been able to reach Jim and that I firmly suspected that he was with someone named Joanne (I wasn't ready to reveal that I really meant "Joe"). I'd read some telephone message from a broken-into trouser pocket. I did that. I'm so bad. I did that. I told the group in the next general meeting. They were ready to bludgeon Jim. They gripped their seats. I didn't even exaggerate. I was furious. They didn't have to be persuaded. I had let the idea that Jim might be gay enter my brain quite often—but then would rationalize it away, until it had the importance of a side dish I wasn't going to eat anyway. Lima beans, maybe.

This grew, this Seventy-eighth Street singing rehab group, for the next few days, and it was sincerely the most fun and the loosest of singing I had been part of in ages. Before I left, I made lots of promises that I never kept, and I still consider my lack of carrying through as a lost opportunity. I really should have, would have, could have carried through.

Jackie said:

"Carly, you have to write it. As a book or a TV show." And then unexpectedly, reflecting the dark side of her humor that I adored, she quipped: "Perhaps you would play the chain-smoker who killed his mother with a sledgehammer."

I laughed aloud. Jackie's humor was a joy to me and her enthusiasm buoyed my spirits. But it also filled me with horror that she might expect more from me than I could deliver. The lines between us were not always sharply defined, but one thing she was very clear about was the subject of Jim. She would insist:

"One thing you have to get clear from your mind is Jim's mystery life." I had only just found the "beard" poem. I'd convinced myself that the description was a disguise—meant to throw me off. My interpretation was set in the broader tableau of betrayals. This was after someone on my team robbed me of a large sum of money and my self-esteem had found new depths. How I would continue to be caught up in the mendacious webs of devious people was beyond me.

Jackie said, "We have to find somebody to handle your money and see that these terrible things don't happen to you." I knew she had fought her way through sharks to get what was hers. I, on the other hand, was a deer in the headlights, wide-eyed, waiting for abuse.

I found the head of the rehab meetings intolerable, and the air quality was getting to my sinuses, and I was being a prima donna and also distrusting Jim. What was he up to? It had been less than ten days, but I wanted out. I said a big dramatic farewell to my friends and called Jim and asked him to pick me up the next morning. Marion, the program's leader, was lashing out at me, ordering me to stay. They didn't take any insurance, and I was a fully paying customer. I could get out if I wanted.

"You don't realize how serious your problem is."

"I don't dispute you, Marion, I just would rather deal with it in another way."

"Well, you little hot shit. You'd leave all these responsible men seeking to get well and you go back to your home and dip into your stash . . ."

"Shut up, Marion. I don't like you."

"Now, that's the voice of yours I've been waiting to hear. That's the real Carly."

I went to my room and packed all my docile soft things and was out of there in half an hour. Like a released bird, I ran into Jim's waiting arms after I was chased by a group of the well-intentioned white-coated men into the elevator.

"What about our singing group?"

"What about your promise to yourself?"

"Are you giving up?"

"You know you're only going to go back to your reckless ways."

"You can't help yourself the way we can help you."

"What about the baritones?"

"Get me the fuck out of here," I said to Jim under my breath.

I called Jackie from the corner, from what was probably the last coin-operated pay phone in all of New York. I was armed once again with my sharps and I could kill people with my nail file if I wanted. I felt embarrassed, but also free. Had they been right? Was I a danger to myself? I hadn't had any of my pills for a week and I didn't notice any symptoms of detox. No shakes or jitters or crawling skin. I did locate all the spots in my apartment where danger lurked. A few old 222s from Canada and some Sinutabs. Sinutabs were an unsung song, one of pleasure and syrupy body motions. The mind slowed down and blurriness replaced overly clear visions of oncoming cars on dark roads.

Yes, it had been Jackie that I spoke to every single night in rehab. Not Jim. But I couldn't tell him that. I told him that when it came time to make the call, I was either meditating or rehearsing with my soul-singing group. Why did I feel the need to keep Jackie a secret from Jim? Was it my addict's behavior? The same impulse that drove me to sneak a chip or a pellet as I savored the secret, delicious aloneness of knowing something others didn't? Or was it simply because it was Jackie, not Jim, who listened with loving-kindness as I told her about the other patients, their stories, and my fears? She loved that I'd formed that soul band in rehab and asked each night what we were rehearsing.

"I never got the manuscript you told me you'd sent over," Jackie mentioned almost casually, referring to the final version of my new children's book, *The Nighttime Chauffeur*, along with Margot's illustrations. Before going into Summer House, I had left the manuscript for Jim to drop off with Jackie's doorman, or ask a nice bike messenger to pedal it across the park to 1040 Fifth Avenue.

"I have no idea what happened," I said, covering. "But I'll find it and get it right over to you."

Jackie was relieved and happy that I was back and she was persistently interested in my experience. "The last time you and I spoke, you had worked up that song—what's it called, 'Chapel of Love'?" she said. "Didn't you sing that at Caroline's wedding? Oh, Carly, rehab sounds like it was almost *fun*!"

"Almost. The jury's out," I told her.

ALTHOUGH SHE HAD TOLD ME she could well understand how and why I loved Jim, she was still unforgiving about our practical union. The first time I told her I discovered his poem to a bearded lover, she said, "Oh, *no*, Carly," as if the contents of the poem proved yet another point she'd been trying to make about him. She told me I should kick him out, which of course I didn't. Was the issue for her that he had no money? Money could make up for so many questionable details, including the alligator-scrotum-covered barstool seats on Aristotle Onassis's yacht. Money could repair and restore almost anything. Should I really be so surprised Jackie believed this, as she was born during the Great Depression to a father who spent much of his life shoveling his way out of debt?

For my part, I never understood money very well. Once when I was seven or eight, I asked my mother how much money my father made. She said, "Do you know how many quarters are in a dollar?" "Four," I said.

"Okay," she said, "now, can you multiply that by one hundred?" It took me a while but I finally said, "Four hundred quarters?" She made it easier for me by reframing the amount as "one hundred dollars." She showed me a dollar bill, explaining that it was the same as four quarters.

"Why is it paper and why are the quarters silver?" was my next question, and she said something about how when the numbers get bigger, it's easier to show the amount on paper. "Imagine carrying four hundred quarters!" She laughed.

"Is that how much Daddy makes—one hundred dollars? Does he make that in a day, or a month, or a year?"

"Actually, Daddy has more than ten thousand dollars."

"So that's what . . . in quarters?"

"I'd have to do some paperwork to get the answer, but let's just say that Daddy has plenty of money."

"Is that why we have a big house? Two big houses?"

"Yes, Carly, that is why we are blessed to have most of the things we want."

"How much is a million dollars, say, in dog years?"

"A million dollars is enough to pay for an airplane or a castle or lots of land or a schoolhouse or lots of cars. Dogs don't care about those things."

This was confounding, confusing, and I could tell my mother was winging it. She didn't know a whole lot more about money than I did.

That was all I got from Mommy on the subject for many years.

Both Jackie and Mike had always been fascinated by my mother. Indeed, Andrea Simon was coined a "German tank" by Mike, who, when he met her for the first time at a gallery opening, was frozen in her presence and afterward told me that my mother was the scariest person he had ever met. Well, I knew she was scary, but what did Mike, of all people, find scary about the dear, diminutive, gray-haired woman with the Katharine Hepburn face and the tiny, twinkling, pale green eyes? Was it all the little stories I'd told him? Like the one about how when Mommy watched a four-minute version of a tape commemorating my twenty years in show business, she said only, "Too much of one person"?

I remember countering, "I would never get tired of seeing Sally or Ben picking at scabs for an hour, if they wanted me to see it."

My mother looked down at her needlepoint. "You'd be surprised. Just wait."

Throughout high school, I was given an allowance, starting at ten dollars a week, and it went up by five dollars every year. In return, I did various chores around the house: weeding occasionally, polishing the cars, cleaning the bathtub, babysitting my brother, and tackling assorted other responsibilities my mother thought would help me get through life. My sisters got more than I did, in deference to their ages, Lucy fifteen dollars and Joey at least twenty-five dollars a week.

By the time I was a senior in high school, my allowance had increased to twenty-five dollars, most of which I spent on petty stuff. Mommy still paid for big-ticket items like dresses, shoes, schoolbooks, and occasionally transportation to New York for shopping; and Daddy's chauffeur, Junius, took me wherever I wanted to go. But getting an allowance was a way of learning how much the world cost.

I never asked my female friends whether they got allowances, or how much, intuiting that for whatever the reason, the topic was best kept shrouded in secrecy. Money was something to be modest about in case they got less, or more, than I did. I knew it could cause jealousy or envy or something unfriendly to erupt and damage a friendship.

When I was in tenth grade, I remember asking my uncle Peter how much money my father made. Uncle Peter took a long pause and answered: "As much as the man in the moon wants to pay him."

"No! Be serious! How much does he make in a year?"

"I really don't know, but it's more than the copper beech tree makes. It's more than John Luckshow, the caretaker, makes, but it's not as much as Porgy and Bess [our two Labrador retrievers] make in a year."

I knew of course that he was still making jokes, and more jokes.

"Carl-pot [Uncle Peter's nickname for me, unless it was Carlsbad the Cavernous One], I just don't know. It probably changes every year. Sometimes it's a hundred and fifty dollars and sometimes it's ten thousand dollars."

"Why do we have such a big house? Is it because he's famous?"

"No—it has to do with the cats. If the cats catch the mice, it can be a big year."

I knew I had to stop talking, quit asking. I would never be able to find out the answer; I'd have to figure it out from life lessons. The truth was that no one really knew unless you were Leon Shimkin, the accountant at Simon and Schuster who first handled the money, then became a partner, and finally kicked my father out of the company he founded, all the while helping himself not only to my father's cash supply but also to the pride of his life.

When my father died, in 1960, it was the beginning of one of my Numb Times, a time when I went inside myself, becoming less and less sure of how I felt. After his death, there was naturally a great deal of sadness, though whose sadness it was I could never be sure. Not my mother's, who I sometimes felt wished that Daddy would die, and whose affair with my brother's tutor had, by then, been going on for eight years. My sisters Lucy and Joey were bereft, though Lucy directed much of her sadness into anger at my mother and her behavior toward our father. As for me, no matter how hard I tried, I couldn't make contact with any pain. My relationship with Daddy had always been remote, had always made me feel so insignificant, and early on I'd stopped trying to win his love.

When he died, the mystery around the money he made deepened. No one ever told me what was in his will. Later, I found out that he had left behind enough money to support his family with—compared to most people—a great deal of ease.

There were two trusts, A and B, containing just under a million dollars apiece. The interest from trust A went to my mother, and the interest from trust B was divided four ways, between me, my sisters, Joey and Lucy, and my brother, Peter. My share came to around $750 a month, and in the sixties and early seventies, that was more than enough money to cover my rent, especially since I lived for a time with my older sister Joey, and she and I pooled our monthly expenses. I continued to receive my share until 1974, when I was cut out of the monthly stipend. I'm not sure who made that decision, but as a result of my marriage to James, and the fact that I was making quite a bit of money at the time from record sales (I had had three hit albums by that point), I was asked to put my monthly income from Daddy's trust back into the pie, which would then be divided among my siblings.

It made sense, I understood completely—Joey and Peter could benefit more from the extra money, and it would have been a crude and stingy thing for me to refuse—but in some illogical, emotional, deeply rooted way, my feelings were terribly hurt. Never having felt like the apple of my father's eye, or even the lychee, I ended up feeling like I belonged even less to my family: the bad seed, ugly duckling, interloper.

I also knew what was coming: I would be removed in part from my mother's will. It was one of the deeper cuts of my life, deeper than what felt reasonable. I already felt guilty about my success.

A month before my mother died, in 1994, I was sitting in the library of her house when her lawyer said he had an important issue he would like to discuss. It seemed that despite my willingness to forgo my share of the trust income after my marriage to James, my mother's will stated I would inherit whatever income I would have received from 1974 to 1994, around $100,000. It was a gesture, the lawyer said, a rather obsequious interpretation. Was it one my mother really "meant" but one she would also prefer I didn't accept? Huh? What did that mean? My mother left me that money in writing, but never meant it? It was a joke all along? Whose idea was this? Did Mother really will me nothing?

However much it hurt, we were all children of privilege, and I knew no one was going to go away ravaged by poverty. It was, as Jake would say, a problem of the rich. Rich people were sometimes the worst, outdoing each other at every million-dollar turn. I wouldn't be affected, I told myself. Yet no matter how relieved I was by the bottom line of my checking account, the slight might as well have been the extra hotdog Mommy gave Joey rather than me; the boy who liked Lucy and not me; the father who didn't think I was pretty. I felt nothing but sad, furious, and suspicious. At the same time, as they rationalized our mother's request, they put their arms around me and told me they loved me and they'd never hurt me. I'm pretty sure if I'd been in their place I would have acted as they did. In fact, we came through it because we could see ourselves in each other and had to forgive the humanness that created the greed and, in my case, the inability to overcome the power of the past. They are so much my blood and I theirs. Each of them is every bit as talented as I am, and it's only timing and luck that brought me out in front of a public audience in a more visible way. I point out to my siblings often enough that there are no divorces in their families, and they have more stable nervous systems. But the currency that twisted itself into occasional bitterness was wealth and fame. I have always wondered if guilt over my variable success wasn't part of why I shied away from going on stage. I felt broken, and torn from my family.

Maybe it was into that very tender breach that Jackie stepped.

We have no secrets

We tell each other everything

About the lovers in our past

And why they didn't last

—"WE HAVE NO SECRETS"

8

Fairy Princess
in a Spin Cycle

I T WAS CHRISTMAS OF 1988 when Jackie asked me if I
had heard *Never Die Young*, James's most recent album.
I answered her honestly, that no, I hadn't listened to it,
with the exception of the title song, and that I would have
to be alone in my car with no one else around in order to
do so. "I told you *I* would listen to it and, well, Carly, it's so
interesting, you know I just really paid attention to that first
song. I read the lyrics and I thought very hard about it . . ."
Jackie let this thought go. "What does it mean to you?

What I mean is, what does hearing your husband, who is no longer . . . here, you know, no longer in your life . . . what does it make you feel?"

Oh, it was so tender ("sweet," as Jackie would say). I wondered if she had said the word "dead" to herself before editing it and going for the euphemism instead. *No longer in your life.* I thought of the thousands of times we, the people in this country, and on this planet, have heard the voice of JFK being electronically recalled. I wanted to say something but got stuck. Jackie picked up the thread and, as she so often did, switched to a third person, impersonal way of speaking.

"I think . . ."—Jackie spoke very slowly—"one is always on guard . . . I mean, you don't know when you go into a grocery store, if you'll hear that song. And you must think . . ." And then, as she often did, she became hesitant, aphasic. She would almost complete her sentence and, unable to find or decide on the word, begin a new one. "You would think . . . those words about 'circle around the sun' . . . I know that you used to sing that song, also, and then the poooo-etry"— Jackie elongated the word—"in that line that describes the two of you . . . 'They're a little too sweet, they're a little too tight . . . not enough tough . . .'"

I know that I leaned over and gave her a tentative, formal, quick hug.

What on earth could I say? Had I ever made such a comparison, or put it together that despite the huge and obvious differences between them, we both had had husbands who were "gone" for us, yet whose voices remained? To have an important part of your life reduced to an easy song, even if it was the title song on a personal album, was akin in some far-fetched ways to Jackie's own experience. It's almost impossible to conceive. Perhaps she really felt an alliance.

"James used to sit on the edge of my bed writing songs," I told her. "I particularly remember him composing 'Secret O' Life.'" When I told her this, Jackie smiled.

"I was just thinking," she said, "that Jack would sit on the edge of my bed when he was going over his inauguration speech and perfecting it and he'd ask me what I thought." She and I laughed at the synchronicity, the obvious self-congratulation that some people would read into the scene.

How did it feel to hear "one's husband's" voice on the radio? I couldn't take the leap and ask her that question in return. Not then, at least. I would wait for when and if she brought it up more directly. This was no doubt a quandary for many of Jackie's friends, and though I can't be sure, I had sensed that Bunny Mellon, perfect in every way, would have known when to press, and follow up, and when to remain silent.

Instead, I said, "Did I ever tell you that James and I have the same rising sign—astrologically speaking, that is? Something about our moons being seventeen degrees in Aries? I don't know what it says about our connection, but it seems as if maybe James was referring to that statistic when he sings, 'synchronized with the rising moon, even with the evening star' . . . "

I wanted to hit myself the minute I said it. How trivial I was. The gatekeeper would need a fierce talking-to.

"'True love written in stone,'" Jackie said. She paused and then continued with her analysis: "'One must be so close to the flame to be alive.'"

Could this really be happening? Our conversation was not that different from two girls coming home from school with the latest album and slipping it out of its sleeve, fitting it on the turntable, and devouring and dissecting every speck of cover art and every word in the liner notes as we examined and attempted to analyze every single turn of every single phrase.

IT WAS EARLY 1991 OR '92, springtime on the Vineyard. Late May, late morning, nearing noon, and I was off to Jackie's house in Aquinnah for lunch.

The morning had come up hoarse, the windows of my house misted over with humidity, with no imminent relief of rain to clear the air. The air lay there, befogged, as if the breezes couldn't make up their minds in which direction to stream, coming in instead from all four directions, and every other direction in between. Altogether an unsteady start to the day.

From my house in Lambert's Cove I took the slower,

more delicious route "up-island," signifying the section of the Vineyard where the towns don't groove and holler with stores and restaurants. Up-island is the quiet part of the Vineyard, with only a fishing village, a few rustic boutiques, a general store, and my favorite fish market, Poole's, where residents lined up to eat oysters raw while balancing their Bergdorf bags in their salty paws. It's also where I spent my summers growing up, with my family, and, when I was fifteen, with my boyfriend, Nick, who drove a fish delivery truck.

I picked up some shrimp in Menemsha, then continued down North Road. By now the fog had lifted and I admired the trees that were at their glorious best, each one revealing its blooms on a private timetable. Some were hardly showing at all, while others revealed a shy light green, like butterflies against the silhouettes of other trees only days more mature, slightly darker or bluer. Over this impressionistic canvas, the oaks, the locusts, the beetlebungs, the maples, the beeches, and the birch trees stood in reflection against the high hedge evergreens. Finally, tossing in a carelessly romantic flourish was the full bloom of the shad, holding forth like a fairy princess in a spin cycle.

I must remember to tell Jackie all of this, I thought. Jackie, who loved any and all descriptions of nature. I took a left turn through a gate leading to the long driveway to Jackie's house, which was perched in a safe spot at a distance from the ocean and the beach, lest the water do what all our conservationist friends, including Teddy Kennedy, promised it might someday do. Jackie's brother-in-law was a longtime proponent of preserving lighthouses, combating erosion, improving water quality, and addressing so many other valuable things. It was something of a surprise that Jackie had decided that the remote end of the island was to be the site of her home. It was in the middle of the Native American reservation, far from the hospital, airport, and ferry. Isolated.

Just as I was turning in the driveway to park, I heard a very familiar intro to a song on the radio that at first I couldn't identify. Maybe it was a song by Simply Red or Crowded House? Then the vocal began. It was James singing *It used to be her town* . . . I mean, *fuck*. I sat there, listening to the whole thing. I even sang along with it. What on earth?

Throughout the eighties and nineties, I had seen James now and again, mostly when he picked up Ben and Sally, then sped away in his little silver car. We, all of us, were still looking for a rapprochement with him and finding not even a single signpost. I was always so dumbly hopeful, over-analyzing or reading too much into every moment, tender or not, lest I catch the wrong wave. Our encounters were a combination of moments to mute and chill the soul, followed, when I least expected it, by sweet, memorable ones. Why were both equally wrenching to me?

Last night was Sally's 19th birthday at Orso, I wrote in my diary around that time.

James joined us. It was so much fun, and on the way
home in the cab with Ben, me, and James, a song came
on the radio, some 1970s-era tune. "Gosh, there I am on
the radio again," I said, kidding. "Oh, I thought it was
James Taylor," the cabdriver said, not recognizing James
in the back seat. Then, "Do you ever talk to him?" "Not
very much," James broke in, adding, "Not enough." The
cabdriver said something complimentary about James's
music and I said, "Yeah, well, he's ... he's ... OK," and
all four of us shared secretive smiles in the back of the cab.
That was a first: communicating dishonestly through
cabdrivers.

ANOTHER TIME IN THE MID-NINETIES, midsummer,
midday, I was alone in the Vineyard house when James
showed up unexpectedly. It had been our home together for
so many years, it would have seemed natural for him to walk
the halls and go look for what he was looking for without having to communicate with me. He was picking up Ben's Rollerblades. The TV was on and I didn't hear him come in the
back door. I was smoking a cigarette (a habit I had publicly
quit) when I heard a noise and went searching for its source.
There was James, a Rollerblade in each hand. I wondered:
who was the most vulnerable person in this house? The most
dangerous? Who was the intruder? We didn't embrace, surrounded as we were by the wrong furniture, weighed down

by history, history that had an uneasy subtext. I remembered the fight we had over when to move Ben's crib into that room and where to place the baby monitor.

For the next half hour, I experienced the highest level of awkwardness. We talked about the easy things at first: the fallen willow, kids' photos on the wall, work pressures, financial pressures, how the Vineyard had changed since we had built this house. Not how the house had changed. That would have been too intimate. Then he broke the unspoken rule of staying bland:

"Mirth has left me . . . at a time when I should be happy because I am single."

A shock wave passed through me. Who the hell did he think I was? Mirth? Left you? When was mirth a part of the rule book? Discussing his mirth? It was like mentioning a visit to the proctologist. His comment brought me back to the familiar part of myself that always revealed more than I should have. I said, "Just know that wherever you are, there is somebody here who quietly loves you forever."

There was a long, strained silence. I looked straight into his eyes and he moved away from my asking face. He shifted back to indifference, having left it only long enough to elicit my declaration of love. He then asked me how long I would be on the Vineyard. He stood on the stairs, with me on the landing above him, my hair hanging down over the bars of the banister. I thought: These sentimental complications are part of our landscape now, but James Taylor, your indifference is no match for my love. You come into my house as though you know you still own it. You do own it, but it's not the house.

"You really are a sweetheart," he said, to fill the empty air. It was then I thought of Mike saying to me: "When you're feeling unloved, play loved."

I smiled and stood up straight.

He left through the door he had come in, disappearing, with the Rollerblades, into the overly humid summer day.

When he was gone, I felt defeated, silly, and in love, but those were not unfamiliar emotions. It was like learning to live with a disease, or the loss of a limb. That "half of myself" feeling is, just maybe, one of the themes of my life.

MARTA SCUBIN was not just Jackie's truly dear, smart, and talented cook and housekeeper, but also a close friend to her whole family. She greeted me at the front door. She told me "Madame" was waiting with tea and crumpets on her flagstone porch, the one looking out over the pond that required a short kayak or rowboat ride, or a muddy walk past in order to reach Jackie's big, beautiful, almost empty beach. Egrets, yes. Gulls, yes. People, no. Except for family, Jackie never liked having a lot of people around her. Unless they were off to the right, and at quite a distance—one whose sighting would require a muscular pair of spyglasses.

A few minutes later, Jackie and I were settling down in our chairs, getting comfortable. She wore a bathing suit, with a simple sarong around her waist, and I was in mid-thigh shorts and a tank top. We were both wearing our wampum bracelets that Kate Taylor, James's sister, had made. I got mine first, and Jackie told me she adored it, so of course I called Kate, who made one for Jackie in record time. Jackie's was just a little more gorgeous than mine, which was only right.

I told Jackie about hearing James's voice on the radio on the way up to her house. She went straight to the heart of things:

"Will you ever understand such an interception?" she asked. Her choice of words was "perfect," I told her, "brilliant": an *interception*. I was so appreciative that Jackie was able to get so quickly to the essence of what I was feeling. I thought, Yes, friends should be able to reveal themselves like characters in a novel you love, otherwise what's the point of having them?

"I was reeled in when I wasn't expecting it," I told her, adding that of course I had to listen all through to where James sings, *She gets the house and the garden, he gets the boys in the band.*

"It's as though the universe knew you'd be in the car at that time and it wanted to test you. I don't know . . ." She paused. "Maybe it was *cunning*. It seems as though certain songs follow me around, too, like 'Greensleeves,' which I've told you was Jack's favorite song."

ANOTHER TIME IN THE EARLY YEARS of our friendship, away from the Vineyard in a restaurant in New York, after another long lunch that stretched into the early evening, I had a spur-of-the-moment thought. Would Jackie like to come back to my apartment for tea? She'd come over before, but it would certainly be the first time she had been there without my getting it ready for her. As we entered through the kitchen door into my old-school, paint-chipped, high-ceilinged, rent-controlled, dozen-room abode with its messy kitchen, shabby curtains, and oddly paired fabrics pulled together from assorted old houses, I naturally focused exclusively on all the uncomely elements and eyesores. School notebooks, Ben's exotic motor toys, dog playthings, and not overly fresh-smelling dog food unwashed from its bowl. There were also intrusions of scarves and gloves that had been flopped here, there, and everywhere over the past few months.

"This is just what I love about the way you make your home feel." Jackie swooned. "It's really . . . natural, and well, 'friendly' wouldn't be quite the right word, but still it has a charm that's so particularly 'you.' I mean, Bunny would never have, oh, say, positioned the carton of milk on the counter just so, but . . ."

No, she was kidding, right? She wasn't going to simultaneously make fun of the milk carton while also putting it in a positive artistic light. Was she?

Jackie had done this before—called attention to a completely mundane assemblage of my pots and pans distributed in a—what's the best way to describe it?—an "artsy" way. Regarding my aesthetic, wasn't she really saying, *Carly, it's so sweet how completely messy you are*? No. That wasn't like her, to be a phony. Oh, she could phony it up (we all could), but she knew I would have caught it. No. "Oh, look, how charming, the bed's not made, how quaint, all your clothes are left on the floor!" are some of the things she didn't say, and wouldn't have said without a wink, about the collective selvedges of drapes, clothes, makeup, and bedclothes she had to walk over and through. I remembered the well-publicized fact that Jackie made her kids clean their own rooms and pick their clothes up off the floor.

It had been raining, and we took off our soaked outer clothes, leaving them on the backs of the kitchen chairs. It seemed that Sally and Ben had had a friend or friends over that day, and loud, restless punk music came from their rooms. Well, I was pretty sure that Jackie's son John didn't listen to a whole lot of Mozart or Duke Ellington, either. In fact, I was very much in sync with Sally and Ben's musical tastes. We all listened to and loved the Stones, the Beatles, Cat Stevens, Nina Simone, Neil Young, Bonnie Raitt, Aretha, sixties Motown, Andreas Vollenweider, and others. I was also pretty sure I didn't want to knock on their bedroom doors and intrude on a bunch of school friends busy downing, along with their hosts, a bottle of the hormone-animating Johnnie Walker.

I asked Jackie if she wanted some tea and in turn she asked for the "powder room," and I led her down the hall to the bathroom—ring around the tub, towels on the floor, not to mention Sally's powder, hair clips, and other paraphernalia befitting a teenage girl. I returned to the kitchen to set up a little tray with two cups and saucers, some Earl Grey tea bags, teaspoons, sugar cubes in a little bowl, and skim milk in a pitcher. I had forgotten entirely about the hot water.

I soon heard Jackie walking back up the long hallway, pausing every few feet to glance at the two dozen or so photographs lining the walls. She'd seen them all before, but her fascination was not politesse. I truly think she was hungry for details she'd forgotten from past visits. There were the usual Simon family photos, taken mostly by my father and my brother, Peter, black-and-white and displayed in uniform three-quarter-inch frames. Another thing that might have been a nice surprise for Jackie? There was no art. Nothing on the walls that might have caused her to think, Oh, dear, I think Jayne Wrightsman might have one of those Rothkos, too. I'd better rush out and get one.

I knew that Jackie identified with Jayne and Bunny. But at the same time, there was also another, more curious and attractive sensibility at play. Jackie was, at heart if not in appearance, a bohemian. She was attracted to the unconventional. She was someone who loved sneaking out with me to smoke a cigarette in the middle of the opera, the two of us kneeling down to extinguish our half-smoked butts for the purpose of relighting them at the next intermission. Even if we ended up in a place where it was perfectly legal to smoke, Jackie always made the whole thing feel illicit in a furtive, adolescent way. And if someone came up to ask her for an autograph, she could be rather abrupt when she said, "Not now," or "No, that's all right, thank you." She had the attitude of "why would anyone want my autograph? Shoo."

She never said it the way a royal would. The words were succinct, a gruff statement of fact (her First Lady voice?) that sometimes made me feel bad for the person asking. In the years I knew her, I never saw Jackie sign a single scrap of paper. She had done it enough times and she had decided at one point she would never do it again. Other times she punted the question over to me: "Carly, you sign *your* name . . ." in a low whisper under one hand. Whenever we were out together and someone spotted her—at the opera, say, or just walking down the street—Jackie would always pretend people were staring at *me*.

"They're all trying to get a good look at you, Carly," she would whisper as we took our seats at the Met. Once when we were swimming off Maurice's yacht on the Vineyard, an airplane began flying low, as if trying to get a photo.

"Look, Carly," Jackie called out, "they're trying to see you in the boat!" Did she think for one second I would ever fall for that? Still, the deflection was charming and for the briefest of seconds flattering, before I reminded myself of the absurdity of it all. As the world knows by now, Jackie disliked being the center of attention. In her presence, I never remembered or accepted the fact that I was a well-known person in my own right. In my own field. But compared to hers, my field was a small garden of roses in the middle of the Amazon rain forest.

I ended up boiling plenty of water for those Earl Grey tea bags, and as we drank tea and spoke intimately over the bass-heavy soundtrack coming from Ben's and Sally's rooms, afternoon drifted into evening. When Jackie left through the kitchen door, the milk carton was still in its place.

WHAT'S PLAYING on the East Side? What's playing on the West Side? Uptown? Downtown? What's playing at the Roxy? Whenever we both happened to be in New York at the same time, Jackie and I made plans to go to the movies. In those days, if you didn't have a newspaper handy, you called 777-Film to find out what was playing and where and at what time, and that's how I stumbled into a little inconvenient web of cross-purposes.

I'll tell you what was playing uptown, downtown, and at the Roxy: *JFK*. It was early in 1992, a few months after the release of Oliver Stone's conspiracy-minded unpacking of the Kennedy assassination, and the movie was still playing at various theaters. How could we stay as far away as possible from a *JFK* sighting, from seeing even a poster, the one with Kevin Costner glaring through an American flag wearing his horn-rimmed glasses? The human eye would always seek out the much smaller photo at the top of the poster, of the motorcade, the chaotic aftermath. Maybe, just maybe, the eye could redirect the moment, make things work, subvert destiny. The eye can somehow keep the shots from ringing out, and have the happy, beautiful couple return to Washington after a day at the races in Dallas, Texas.

And what about the previews? Scarier, even, would be a minute-long trailer for *JFK* inserted before the feature-length film we'd gone to see. That one minute could end up destroying the entire afternoon.

"You pick out the movie," Jackie had said, "and I'll meet you there."

I did so much homework, did so much to head off any possible encounter with *JFK*. I amused myself by imagining my extremely serious CEO voice demanding to speak immediately to the owner of the Sony cinema complex at Lincoln Square, telling him I needed "highly important and classified information." Well, from all the intelligence I was able to extract, I learned that *Bugsy*, starring Warren Beatty and Annette Bening, was the only movie in town that wasn't surrounded by other theaters that might have been playing

JFK and that was playing at a time that was good for both of us. When I called her back, Jackie was happy with the choice, and she and I had a quick Warren Beatty moment, since he had been a mutual acquaintance. We also talked about Annette Bening, and how interesting a person she must be. I gave Jackie the address, Second Avenue and Sixty-fourth Street, and she seemed satisfied with the arrangement.

Jackie and I usually met up at the movies in the same way. When she arrived before me, I would find her inside the movie theater by going to the ladies' room, where she would be waiting in one of the stalls. That afternoon, at the 4 p.m. showing of *Bugsy*, was no different. Her Gucci loafers were poking out from beneath a stall. I hummed a bar of a familiar song, in this case "How High the Moon," which was the signal for *all clear*.

Jackie emerged. "I almost thought the woman who came in a minute ago was you, and I . . . it wouldn't have been the worst thing, but . . . well, shall we go in? Oh, Carly, I see you got popcorn . . . what *fun*!"

We took an elevator and arrived at theater number two, finding nothing to fly in the face of a happy Thursday afternoon spent seeing *Bugsy* with your girlfriend. The theater was mostly empty, with maybe twenty other people distributed like arbitrary commas in the semidarkness. We took off our coats and put them on the seat next to us. Even though I had averted a major faux pas, I still felt terribly ill at ease.

There hung between us a palpable silence, and for some reason I couldn't allow it. Maybe it was only three seconds, or not even two, but the silence whipped at me like some sudden freak storm. I turned to her, this friend, this woman whose burden it was to be poised, and whose responsibility it was to set an example for the rest of us.

"So," I said, "have you seen *JFK*? I mean the movie. I mean the Oliver Stone movie. I mean the one that's just out now?"

"Oh *no, Carly, no.* No, no." Jackie reacted as if she had been attacked. "It's so awful. *No.*"

I continued my crash into the reef of self-destruction. "I didn't even *mean* to say that," I said. "I just . . ."

"*No, Carly*, NO." She slumped backward into her seat.

That was the end of the conversation about anything and everything *JFK*. I was dead. I couldn't live past this moment. Rewind! Oh, please, rewind!

I started to cry, and I was fortunate to be able to hide it behind the opening music of *Bugsy*, which had just started up. I sat there motionless, shocked silly. "I'm so sorry, Jackie," I whispered.

From my diary on that day: *What sort of brain derangement sent such a signal to my wayward tongue?*

I could hardly concentrate on *Bugsy*. All the while I was thinking: I have to be so careful . . . She is so much more fragile than we all think. Every time a shot sounded on the screen—and the film was plenty violent—she reacted physically, dramatically, her body mimicking the victim. All I wanted to do was protect her, put my arms around her.

I WAS REMINDED that day of the story of Mr. Nose, which is really a story about where a person's best intentions can land. Mr. Nose, as he came to be known forever by my family after this fateful evening, was the unsuspecting man with a prominent nose which we—my sisters and I—were told by our parents *not* to call attention to one night when Lucy was five or six and I was even younger. He was one of my father's erudite authors, and when he showed up, it was true: his nose was not charming, but it was also way too long to *not* notice. That night, I watched it happen. When our father introduced the man to us, Lucy held out her hand and said in her most beguiling voice, "How do you do, Mr. Nose?"

Daddy very quickly led him away from us kids, and I have no idea what happened after that, but the story of Mr. Nose does get a lot of play in the family folklore, an old standby that gets repeated frequently at Thanksgiving and Christmas dinners. Nothing could have been a purer repeat of the essence of the Mr. Nose story than what happened to me at *Bugsy*.

When the movie ended, Jackie gave me a lift home in her Communicar. Again and again I thought to apologize once more, but I also knew it couldn't be done. I knew only that I would never bring that subject up again. So many subjects to be avoided. It was the reason why it was so hard to be as close to her as I wanted to be. When I got back to my apartment, I wrote Jackie a long letter, telling her about Mr. Nose, and sent it to her office by messenger the next day. She called me directly after getting it. "Carly," she said, "no one else would ever have been so upset or as sensitive as you were. I completely understand. I love Mr. Nose"—she laughed—"and someday you should write a children's book about him." She laughed again, and reassured me again, as a good mother would have. I still couldn't get over how I had transgressed, even though it may have been more traumatic for me than it was for her.

Part of my relationship with Jackie was trying to stay out of harm's way. I suffered from a terrible stutter as a child. And while learning to sing helped keep it in check, it is an affliction I carried into adulthood. Thinking before you speak, that natural pause, turns out to be a creature comfort that a stutterer can't always afford. It's complicated, because it has everything to do with being afraid that if I don't say something immediately, I'll begin anticipating what I'm going to say and therefore induce my stutter. My stutter certainly casts a long shadow. Is it mechanical? Do I have certain neural connections that are shorter and stubbier than most people's?

I've thought many times about that night at the movie theater where I watched as my foot landed in my mouth. I knew it was—it must have been—important for Jackie to keep the luster of Camelot alive, at least the version of it she later reported to Arthur Schlesinger. For her own sake. For her children's sake. For the sake of her religion. If it was true that she had convinced Joseph Kennedy, the family patriarch, to persuade his son that she, Jackie, would make the perfect presidential wife, then Jackie had allowed her life and her heritage to be stamped in eternity with that light.

JFK, as well as all the other crass pop culture productions intent on dissecting and distorting her life, must have been terribly disorienting. After Bobby Kennedy was killed, almost nothing could be kept in its respectable place anymore. Perhaps the perfect diversion for her, as it was for more than a few women I've known well, was to abandon some relationship to the "spiritual" and veer 1,000 percent toward the material. To feel comfortable. To feel free to spend as much money as will force all the unbearable pain down to a level you can deal with. Not to give a damn anymore what anyone else thinks or says. It was an issue of sheer survival. On some level Jackie knew that I understood this, which is why, as time went on, it seemed like she felt freer and freer to talk about her past, even if only in little glimpses.

Once Jackie told me, "It will take many generations to

arrive at the kind of equality—if it ever comes—that undoes the idea that women are the smaller, weaker of the sexes, and that women have to rule with a craftiness their mates must know nothing about. The woman is clever and circuitous, isn't she? A man is straightforward and stupid. The hairy ape."

I couldn't help but think of Ari and wonder if she was in some sly way referring to him.

From my second- and thirdhand knowledge, Ari always seemed like a sybaritic and slothful rogue—yet Jackie had also described him as a devastatingly attractive man, who used to sing Argentinian songs to her. I knew about his secret oil fields, his smashing of plates around other wives and lovers, knew about the unsubstantiated rumors that he'd had Bobby Kennedy killed. It was all too rich for me and, I suspect, infinitely so for Jackie. She had to protect herself by putting on a new set of blinders. But I knew this much: I would not have let Jackie marry Ari if I had known her at the time. I would have done something to disrupt their courtship. Oh, *of course* I wouldn't have! Who am I kidding? And, of course, Jackie would have softened under the magnetism of Ari's gaze, and the sheer comfort of the life raft he threw out into the seas, which she so expertly reached out to and caught.

I also remember Jackie telling me that Ari was fierce, filled with illusions of supremacy. But when Ari's son, Alexander, died at the age of twenty-four from injuries suffered in a plane crash, he became convinced he was being punished for his hubris. His guilt closed in on him. It was like the fall of the house of Atreus in Aeschylus's *Oresteia*. Glimpsing his own mortality, he realized he needed to become even richer, even more powerful, to combat the prospect of death. Thankfully, Jackie didn't live to know that her son would die in the same way as Ari's.

"One is overwhelmed by the necessity to cover up the sentiments that are needed in order to go forward with one's life. I had to make such a grand left turn so as not to be reminded of my former life," Jackie explained.

"The life would have to be so completely different," I offered, "like landing on the surface of a different planet."

Jackie continued, "I wondered if I went to the trouble of removing signs, newspapers, photographs, mementos . . . never mind. He wouldn't have seen it clearly, but the reminders were walking every day with me in the bodies of my children. Their walks, their mannerisms, the memories of their births. First words, skating, riding, greetings, nightmares, Christmases, birthdays . . . worries that A.O. [this was how Jackie sometimes referred to Ari] could never erase."

Even if Ari might have been sensitive about spending time with Jackie's children, taking them for walks around his island, Skorpios, or ushering them up to the helm of the yacht and letting them press a button now and then, I could only imagine Jackie holding back tears. Had her original gratitude toward him for saving her turned to a sour, fierce resentment?

It has been written that his son's death was the breaking point in Ari's feelings for Jackie. He was no longer in love with her, and her manners and grace were rendered paltry, even ridiculous. In the face of the rude comments he directed at her, sometimes even in front of guests, Jackie, as a result, spent less time with Ari in Greece. His feeling of abandonment led him to retribution: more public meanness, more allusions to her overspending, and then there were the undisguised, bull-like flirtations with other women—anything to get back at her. No one could hide such strong feelings. They come out. They just do.

Jackie would toss off his behavior with cool aplomb. Still, when Ari initiated divorce proceedings, he continued to want to protect her. In effect he told his lawyer, *I love her and I want you to be very fair.*

"In the beginning," I remember Jackie telling me once, "Ari had a way of 'casting' one. As if you were in his own private Greek mythology. He saw himself as Odysseus, and I was no one to argue. I was so in need of the kind of protection he was offering. I wanted it for Caroline and John. That's what a woman innately knows—she has to protect her children in any and every way, no matter how far away from your innate self you have to go. I fell for that wide net he cast."

Jackie seemed untouched by Ari's crude indiscretions—

his blatant and tasteless womanizing—and she was similarly unbothered by Jack's. She had brought up the subject of Jack's mistresses from time to time with no apparent discomfort or distress. Almost a year earlier, in 1991, she talked about it. In a cheerful but resigned way, she told me that of course she knew about them—she just didn't mind their presence as much as she might have because she knew he loved her more, much more, than any of his dalliances.

Wait, I remember thinking, hearing about all the mistresses, you had to pretend to be blasé? To pretend one was simply used to this in men, because, in Jackie's case, of one's famously handsome and lecherous father? It was Black Jack Bouvier, a poached and distressed drunk, who seemed to have given her the overall license to accept this particular masculine trait. Her father was almost proud of the many women he left in his charming but deadly wake. At least in front of me, Jackie never gave up that half measure of rationalizing the worst, the thing that her Thoroughbred horse friend—me—wouldn't have been able to contain. "I did so terribly much want Jack to be happy," she said once, "and then I couldn't divide myself into the two women I had to be, or had to *act* as if I were."

She told me never to let anyone know how much things hurt. Mike clearly agreed with this philosophy, reminding me to "keep all the cards close to your chest." I can't say that I was able to follow through as much as I would have liked.

I was too attached to the myth that I was "living out my destiny—alone."

Whatever her reasons for marrying Ari, I do know this much: When Ari died in Paris, Jackie's speech before the French press was formal, and without a lot of feeling. She went for scripted, memorized words. "He meant a lot to me. He brought me into a world where one could find both happiness and love. We lived through many beautiful experiences together, which cannot be forgotten and for which I will be eternally grateful."

It seemed to me that Jackie was always looking to give her life over to the care of a stronger man. Maurice Tempelsman appeared after Ari, taking charge of her financial life. After all, he was well versed in the language of diamonds—of mines and caves and undercover dealings. Jackie compared him to the other pirates she had known and loved. Maurice was safe and loving. They were good together.

In the end, what did any of this mean? It was difficult enough to understand as it was. But with aphasia and stammering, fear of overstepping, and carefully working around the truth, it was challenging to really characterize what either one of us was saying, or wanted to say, about love and where it had taken us. I give a lot of credit to the opening-up that each of us, in our own ways, was able to do.

Once, after the annual anniversary of JFK's death had come and gone, along with the surrounding TV and

newspaper stories, I screwed up the courage to write her
about it:

November 29, 1993

Dear Jackie:

*As I now understand, you were to stay in Virginia
until Tuesday. A very sensible thing to do considering
the media coverage, the endless coverage and pounding
beyond reckoning, the merciless going over of the
assassination events. I don't know how you can bear
it. I always wonder how it makes you feel. I can only
imagine that you have to come to some kind of system
of defense or dissociation that enables you to deal with
the reminders. They don't ask you when you want
to be reminded. They just assault you whenever you
innocently turn on the television set, or open a magazine
hoping for a mild diversion. I've thought about this a lot
this past week. I of course could avoid saying this to you
(another reminder), but then there is something, which
is so much there, that is not mentioned. I'm so sorry this
has to be an ongoing part of your life, and I just wanted
to tell you that I love you and have so much respect for
the way you deal with everything. I try to learn from you.
In fact, I don't know anybody who doesn't try to learn
from you. But if you ever want to kick and scream and
shout "No Fair" and fall apart for a minute or a year,
there we will be, understanding that this is the way a*

Great Lady does things. What I am trying to say is that you have an enormous range and never fear exercising it. Naturally, I hope you don't tell me to go to hell for writing you this way!

And soon after,

Dearest Jackie, I am always here for you in any capacity, and I hope you know how dearly I have come to respect your soulfulness. You have more soul than Aretha!

With lots of love, even though this is typed. It may look impersonal, but it's not!

Carly

At the same time, it was difficult to square *that* Jackie— the woman from the books, the woman so central to American history and later global intrigue—with the Jackie in her kitchen on the Vineyard, on the receiving end of an affectionate hug from Maurice after he got back from a long walk or bike ride around the Aquinnah hills. Or the Jackie I once saw diving off the side of Maurice's yacht in her white bathing cap, not at all embarrassed or self-conscious about her exposed flesh. Or the Jackie who did yoga every day on the beach in the summer, and who could, according to our mutual friend Joe Armstrong, who once came upon her during a morning stroll, place both her legs behind her neck. Or

the Jackie who, in between yoga stretches, was a girlishly effusive bummer of cigarettes. Or the Jackie I remember from
the night I shot a music video for one of my songs, "Better
Not Tell Her," from my album *Have You Seen Me Lately?*, on
the beach in front of her Aquinnah house. (It was Jackie's
idea, she who was always suggesting I bring whatever proceedings I had up my sleeve—lunches, get-togethers, musical events—over to *her* house.) I'd hired Latin dancers to
perform alongside the song's Spanish guitar solo. The night
was cool and misty; the only sound, the light crashing of
the nearby waves. At one point, Jackie and Maurice drifted
down from the house, draped in blankets. Jackie had brought
along a thermos of hot chocolate, and I remember how badly
she felt that she hadn't made enough for all the dancers.

My enduring image is of Jackie dancing the tango at my
"Moon Party"—as I called it—which at the time I considered one of the high points of my life, at least socially. It was
a party I hosted in my barn in the summer of 1992 during
a full moon, even though it was pouring lopsided rain over
the enormous white tent I'd had installed over the swimming pool, which, that night at least, had a fountain in it
serving to blend in with the torrent. Most of the usual sus-
pects were there—the Styrons, the Herseys, the Buchwalds,
the Feiffers, the Wallaces, assorted musician friends, as well
as the resident support staff of doctors and lawyers whose
job it was to keep the island bigwigs in good health and their
copyrights from expiring. Jackie came with Maurice. The

dress code was "all white," and guests were invited to sing, or read, or dance anything moon-related. Various Simon and Taylor family members performed, including Sally, doing everything from reciting a self-penned moon-themed poem to singing Van Morrison's "Moondance."

That night, Jackie wore a sleeveless white top over a long full white skirt. Her hair was up in a tight bun and she looked amazingly like photos I'd seen of her father, in all of his Moroccan handsomeness, deep brown tan, wide-set eyes, and gorgeous facial features. Midway through the Moon Party, around the time a few guests began tossing themselves fully clothed into the swimming pool, I spotted Jackie on the dance floor with my close friend Teese Gohl, an amazing Swiss musician and my musical director for twenty years. Teese was teaching Jackie his version of a tango, though Teese told me later he was completely winging it. The two of them, Jackie and Teese, seemed enthralled by the music and by each other. Jackie's motions were as abrupt and delicate as a castanet. Maurice watched adoringly as her entire broad-shouldered body enfolded within the Spanish music, a lone flag gusting and snapping, eternally beautiful in the rhythms of the night. Known by all and by no one.

Don't wake me unless you love me

It takes too long to fall back to sleep

Don't wake me unless you're a friend of mine

I'd rather just fall back on my dreams

—"HAVE YOU SEEN ME LATELY?"

9

The Singular Moment

WITH EVERY PERSON YOU MEET who becomes a loved one, there must be that one brilliant moment. A singular moment when you feel yourself atop a mountain of sequences, one in turn compiled of a thousand other moments, most of them conscious, and electric—shots of pure dopamine through all your synapses. There is that one greatest moment with each friend—each lover—that is the viscerally imprinted one, the one that another doesn't top and shouldn't even try. And the memory of that moment involves up to five senses, each one vibrating at the highest possible frequency. The pinnacle has only one space in the universe, and that place has only *you* as its receiver.

So it was with you, Jackie, the time we were in your bedroom when you said to me, talking of something seemingly unrelated:

"You called me by my name. You see through me." We nearly looked into each other's eyes, but instead, we intently watched the same space in the middle distance. Jackie, like a slightly shaking glass, giving off the rays of a crystal light prism for which she was both deliverer and catcher.

What did it mean? I will remember forever how it felt. In the years since then, I looked everywhere for the other provocative line, "You called me by my name."

The exchange I'm remembering happened in 1993, when we were going over pages of *The Nighttime Chauffeur*, the last children's book Jackie and I did together. She and I were sitting, looking out over Fifth Avenue from her bedroom, a room marked by French provincial furniture with a few discreet touches of India scattered here and there. It was a room belonging to a grown-up, as opposed to the feral undergrowth of houses where small children are underfoot, with that chaos of scuff marks and dog-soaked tennis balls and snack wrappers under the bed. When I arrived, Marta had offered me sherry—a frequent specialty of the house—which I'd accepted. I never drank sherry except at Jackie's apartment.

My mind shot back to a time in 1986, after the release of *Heartburn*, when Mike was having a breakdown of sorts and, having taken the wrong medicine, was badly affected. I was willing but very worried to be his go-to person. Who was I to know what to do? I understood and managed the challenge of finding him a doctor at Presbyterian Hospital in New York, and I bought him an exercise bike for his apartment. I talked it through with his then wife, Annabel, and she seemed only grateful for whatever help I could lend. She and Mike were still very close, but were not living together full-time.

When it was clear that he was circling in his head and in need of immediate hospitalization, I took him with a little suitcase, almost like a child's—like the one that carried my ballet costume to dance class when I was five. As I was standing behind him waiting in line to fill out papers, I looked at this very thin form standing in front of me. His trousers were so loose that, without a belt, they didn't have any chance of staying up around his narrow waist. They slipped a bit, and at the same time I noticed his hair had come a little awry. This, along with the alignment of the pants, was enough to break your heart.

He perseverated over and over, offering one reason after another: What was the catalyst for his fall into mental confusion? What might it be? It must have been this or that. No, that. Oh, Mike. I completely belonged to you. I would never be the same person. We would always have that one frightening moment together that would probably represent, to him, some kind of failure. To me it was singular—that exceptional merging of which only human beings are capable, based on trust and love and triumph over separateness.

BACK TO 1993, sitting with Jackie in her apartment. I knew that Jackie was sick. Leslie's Pharmacy in Vineyard Haven carried all the New York rags, and I'd seen the headlines, read that Jacqueline Kennedy Onassis had been diagnosed with non-Hodgkin's lymphoma. But Jackie never brought it up with me, not directly, and, gripped as always by my fear of trespassing on the personal, I followed her lead. That day, as usual, she focused instead on my material. One of the topics I remember we discussed was the last-minute *errata* slip inside *The Nighttime Chauffeur*, a result of my illustrator, Margot Datz, misreading the text I'd written that referred to a *crescent* moon, drawing instead a full one. At that point, it was too late in the publishing schedule to do anything, and Margot and Jackie had an effective but uneasy confrontation about the mistake. Each stood her ground. Margot's stance was that Jackie, as the book's editor, should have caught the error. And Jackie's stance was that Margot had not been responsible to the text. I stayed neutral, although I suspected that if Jackie had not had a serious illness to contend with, she would, of course, have caught it.

A half hour after I arrived, Jackie said she wanted to show me something and brought out a bound, unlined leather book that she told me she'd made for Aristotle Onassis. She seemed very proud of it. The book was enormous, large enough to cover an entire coffee table. Inside its pages, she told me, she'd copied the entire text of *The Odyssey*, in Greek on one side, and English on the opposite page. There must have been a hundred pages of Jackie's own ink drawings of Ari as Odysseus, depicting his long, siren-filled excursion home, complete with swirling, tsunami-like waves carrying him or, rather, Odysseus, off-course.

The sheer effort—what she'd done—supported the idea of her own fertile imagination feeding the creation of her books at Doubleday. She must have left it on Ari's yacht and later reclaimed it when he was sick in Paris. I don't know what has become of that book, or who got to see it, but I remember thinking it was the most extraordinary gift of love.

Still, the focus that day was on *our* book. As she held it up, Jackie mentioned how beautiful the cover looked. Margot's illustration showed a single aged female passenger in an old-fashioned coach, led by a single, white, high-stepping horse. The night's colors—dark zucchinis, murky pickle-water-greens—were polished and mysterious, exuding an echoing silence, the shaggy branches of trees like a drowned girl's hair, the park and its empty paths and swooping roads lit only by the night sky and a lamppost too far away for comfort from its nearest neighbor.

"Someone—an editorial assistant—told me the other day that the cover looked so much like a dream," Jackie remarked. "Which of course in the book it *is*. A dream of dying and coming back to life again. The idea of the 'night-time chauffeur' as a metaphor for . . ." She didn't finish the thought. "Maybe you hear the jingling and the clop-clop of hooves, and a white horse appears suddenly, out of no-where, and you climb on board and are whisked off into the night . . ."

I had never thought of that take on the book before. The story, at least as I imagined it, was about a little boy, Jasper, whose rocking horse comes to life one night, and his res-cue of an older woman, who by the end of the book is young again. But now I could easily see another interpretation, since Jackie's and my imaginations often traveled along the same perfumed path.

"Do you think you intended that at all when you were writing it, Carly?"

"Not at all, Jackie!" I said, though it was true that at the time my thoughts were focused on death, my mother going in and out of the hospital with one medical crisis after the next, followed by the news about Jackie, which I'd only learned through the most distant side doors.

"Even if you didn't, it's very interesting that someone would say that . . . Especially a younger person, since what do they . . ."

It was then, still looking down at the cover of the book,

she said those words. *You see me, Carly . . . you called me by my name.*

At the time, I assumed the words were from a childhood poem, stanzas she and her classmates were made to memorize at Farmington as part of the school curriculum, or something she remembered from the many books she'd read. *You called me by my name.* A poem that everyone in the world knew by heart—everyone but me, that is—one written by Carl Sandburg or Robert Frost or maybe even Archibald MacLeish, one of those moody, sun-weathered midcentury poets who remained in the greater consciousness. Or else it was a ditty taught by a childhood governess, singsong and eerie. It might even have been a rhyming slogan from a 1950s advertising campaign for sleds, or butter, a tagline heard on TV so many times a day that viewers began humming it over their kitchen sinks.

JACKIE AND I OFTEN quoted our favorite lines of poetry to each other, and once we had a long conversation about one poem by the English poet Stephen Spender. The first line of "The Truly Great" is "I think continually of those who were truly great." It was one of JFK's favorites, if not his most favorite poem, and one he quoted regularly. No doubt Jackie always gave him his due in regard to the poem's unnamed subjects, who, "born of the sun . . .

travelled a short while toward the sun," since unmistakably he was one of them.

There is no question that when I wrote my own song "Touched by the Sun," after learning that Jackie was gravely ill, I borrowed from the Spender poem, both in language and in content. Things were going badly for her. In late 1993, while out riding, she had fallen from her beloved horse, Frank, and in January 1994, a week or so after we'd met at her apartment, we had a long and ultimately curious phone conversation. I was in the bath and it started out as usual—warm and witty and full of references we both understood and embellished along the way. Then, out of the blue, Jackie called me by the wrong name.

"Louisa?"

"Louisa?" I repeated. "This is Carly."

"Louisa?" she said again. Until then it had been so obviously a Jackie-Carly conversation that I knew she had gone to another place in her imagination or catalog of memories. But I glossed over it, ending the conversation hastily by saying I would see her later that week.

When I got out of the bath, I picked up my guitar and started playing, a little angrily, in B minor, a downstroke with a lot of power, while singing, *If you want to be brave / and reach for the top of the sky / and the farthest part of the horizon / do you know who you'll meet there* . . . and then I put in a few names: JFK. Onassis. Martin Luther King. That didn't work at all.

I began singing instead about *great soldiers, and seafarers, and artists, and dreamers / who need to be close / close to the light. They need to be in danger of burning by fire.* I changed key, and went to a high note, since I wanted the melody and lyrics to soar. But I couldn't sing as high as I wanted to go, not naturally, at least, so I sacrificed that first note for one with more of a "striving" quality. I found it, too. *I want to get there / I want to be the one / who is touched by the sun / one who is touched by the sun.* Obviously, Jackie was already touched by the sun, and that calling-out was my wish for myself, maybe, that I could someday be half as radiant or luminous as she was.

I wish I were brave, was my next thought, and the next few lines flowed out: *Often I want to walk / The safe side of the street / And lull myself to sleep / And dull my pain / But deep down inside I know / I've got to learn from the greats / Earn my right to be living / Let my wings of desire / Soar over the night.*

The song was my own little plea to myself: Let me be more like this woman. Let me be who I am and be it all the way and never let my faith leave me.

The rest of the music followed, and by the time I had finished, I'd memorized the chords and sung and played the song to myself over and over again. When Ben came home from the gym that night, I played it for him in the kitchen. He loved it, calling it my "best song ever." Sometime in the next few weeks I recorded a demo. I did not at that time tell Jackie anything about the song.

There had been another sensitive moment where art and life intermingled with Jackie the summer before. We had been at her house on the Vineyard when my album *Have You Seen Me Lately?* came out. There was drama around the making of that album, which I had shared with Jackie. The drama was a result of Meryl Streep in the end not singing the title song because of an altercation between me and Sam O'Steen, the editor of *Postcards from the Edge*, over the song's absence from the opening credits and its consequent departure from the film. I was, of course, terribly disappointed by the loss of the song, but that's showbiz.

Jackie, however, had been livid. It was her "let's get 'em" attitude that tickled me so much. She was like one of the Jets in *West Side Story*—so tough she might have put her dukes up. She couldn't understand how O'Steen had any say in the matter. "Mike should have come to your defense!" she insisted. "The song would have been perfect!" she declared, along with other claims of the song's obvious merits and how it should be in the movie, sung by Meryl in the opening, just as I had intended it to be! Jackie was adamant. We were having a late lunch at her house, and I put on the album at her request. John and Christina Haag, his longtime girlfriend, with whom I had a very warm relationship, were there.

When the song "Life Is Eternal" came on, we noted the Catholic prayer that played a part in the lyrics:

Life is eternal
And love is immortal
And death is only a horizon.
Life is eternal
As we move into the light
And a horizon is nothing
Save the limit of our sight

Then my lyrics went on, another verse reading:

And will I see you up in that heaven?
In all its light will I know you there?
Will we say the things that we never dared?
If wishing makes it so,
Won't you let me know . . .

As the song was playing, John went to answer the phone and returned with the news that his uncle Stephen Smith had died. The song was too close, too much on the mark. Jackie was visibly upset and she began to cry. It was the first time I had ever seen her shed tears. I knew Jackie felt particularly close to the Smiths.

OVER THE YEARS, Jackie and I had talked about extended and immediate family matters. I had told her so much about my family and how growing up, I'd always been incredibly proud of my mother's beauty. I didn't realize it when I was a child, but she was also sexy. She exuded a charismatic, pleasing energy, and I often lingered at school whenever she picked me up, pretending I had an unfinished chore, so that people would have more time to see her.

Over the past few years, my mother's health had started to decline. First there was a renal aneurysm, followed by increasing confusion. I remember once, when she was in bad shape and had "soiled" herself, I carried her through the crowded lobby of the Falmouth Inn, where we had stopped on the way from the hospital in Boston to the ferry. Although she had only almost made it to the bathroom, she had emerged 80 percent cleaned up and exhausted. Anyone else would not have wanted to be seen. But my mother somehow still had just enough energy to call out over my shoulder in her perfect Kate Hepburn tones, "You all know my daughter, Carly Simon, the singer, don't you?"

My relationship with my mother began with my terrific need for her, followed by even more need, followed by my feeling of being rejected by her, followed by her feeling rejected by me. Then came anger and resentment, accompanied by my guilt for feeling like such an unworthy, ungenerous daughter. I felt like I pushed her away over and over again. At one point, she wrote me a letter expressing her pain. She felt excluded from my life, she said, and mortified by that exclusion. I realized why I was so embarrassed whenever I would say I was going over to Jackie's, or that I'd been invited to the White House, or was commiserating with Mia Farrow about Woody Allen. Even just mentioning dinner with our best friends "Mike and Diane" may have sounded to her as if I was showing off. I wasn't. At the same time, I didn't want to make her feel left out, or in any way "less than." "Most of us when we do a caddish thing harbor resentment against the person we have done it to," W. Somerset Maugham wrote in *Cakes and Ale*.

My mother had made a couple of stabs at asking me to ask Jackie over to *her* house, also on Martha's Vineyard. "I'd love to meet her. I'm sure she'd enjoy it, too!" I never repeated the open invitation to Jackie. I would never have put pressure on her like that. Doing that made me feel even guiltier. I was being withholding, very possibly selfish and snooty. I was thinking more about Jackie's sensitivity than my mother's very real desire to get close to the hot hearth of the culture, that imaginary boiler room where the gears of power and money and eternity whirred and clanked and the flames were enough to burn you.

I also recognized that Mommy wasn't being fair or, for that matter, truthful. Why didn't she ever ask me if other friends of mine, lesser mortals, could drop by her house? Why was it *only* the Clintons and Jackie? Of course, I knew the answer. I'm not totally ignorant, nor will I ever forget my father's response when asked once, "Why are so many of your friends celebrities?" His response was, "They're more interesting!" My mother undoubtedly discovered this on her own, or else she came to absorb Daddy's point of view. As for why my parents thought that, well, it derived from the most universally shallow of reasons. Press agents knew, even demanded it, as they would place their young starlets newly on their roster next to Cary Grant.

The night I hosted the Clintons at my house, my mother called me. "Why wasn't I included? Why didn't you invite *me*?"

"Because I was asked please not to have anybody but my immediate family since it was so last-minute, and so informal, and even the time they were supposed to arrive kept changing."

"But I *am* a member of your immediate family!"

"I know, Mommy, but please understand it wasn't a decision I was free to make."

When I told Jackie about this later, she understood. "What a painful bind you were put in," she said. "I know that kind of jealousy happens. With my sister, there was always the one-upmanship. It was predictable and inevitable. I made her so mad she used to try to outdo me. And she did!"

My mother called again the next day, and this time she was in tears. The salespeople at the grocery store had asked her what it was like to meet the Clintons, what she thought of them, whether they were enjoying their vacation on the Vineyard. "I couldn't give them an answer. I was so devastated!"

"Mommy," I said for the third or fourth time, "I couldn't. I wasn't even given the chance." That was how we left it, but I'm not sure she ever forgave me.

At the same time, she was my mother! The Mommy who held me upright when I was an infant unable to keep milk down. The Mommy who held me on her lap when I was too nervous to go to school for any variety of psychosomatic reasons. The Mommy who told me I had a great voice, a voice that carried and carried, and someday I might be a really good singer. Yes, she said some awful things, too, but when she got sick, suddenly they didn't matter. She had done so many things so right, with whatever skills, emotional and otherwise, she had at the time. I loved my mother. I also *understood* her, and knew what she wanted from me, so why was I so reluctant sometimes to give it to her? Was I getting some perverse revenge for the things or attention I hadn't gotten as a child? "Don't be hard on yourself," Jackie kept insisting. But I always will be. I wish I'd had forethought.

But it was true that any time my mother got sick, or an accident befell her—like the time a swarm of bees chased her hands off the steering wheel of her car, propelling her straight into a scrub oak on South Road on the Vineyard—I would be by her side. To help her, of course, but also from the fear that our positions had reversed, struggling not to revert to my earliest position as a completely dependent child. And whenever I had a bad anxiety attack, whether I was across the ocean or three miles away, Mommy—not my doctor, not my two sisters, not my dog or my bed—was my go-to source of relief. It was always my mother's arms I sought. I would wrap myself in them, only to be stung a day later by a poisonous comment that pushed me back out to arm's length. I would be angry and shocked at myself that I could simultaneously be so infantile and, just as quickly, so furious and cold.

Throughout the late 1980s and early 1990s, my mother would call: "Oh, darling, I never see you! Come visit! Please! I have some Mott's applesauce and some nice cream of mushroom soup. I'll pay for you to take a cab."

She would always get me with that cab offer. It took twenty minutes to travel from Central Park West to Riverside Drive, then up the Hudson Parkway to Riverdale. Mommy and I would spend a few hours averting petty arguments, and she would ask me about Cat Stevens, forgetting I had done plenty, lived plenty, since that time. She would say things I would try my hardest not to get irked by: the time before my wedding to Jim when she told Lucy, "You *never* give a present to the bride at her second wedding." When I got engaged to my first husband, James, in 1972, instead of giving me the antique table that had been in our dining room when I was growing up—that I'd asked for when she asked what I *really* wanted—she gave me a used *Encyclopædia Britannica*.

On one of those visits, I wrote in my diary afterward:

Angry at her jaw clicking while she ate cereal mixed with
Jell-O, milk, and bananas for over half an hour. She did
this while telling lies. Click, lie, click, click, lie, lie, click,
lie and so forth. I still see her in myself every time I click
and notice Sally noticing it.

After a few hours of soup, I would go home in the second cab she hadn't paid for.

The day before Mommy died, in early 1994, I remember
looking at her body on her bed, thinking that she was sleep-
ing too soundly for actual sleep. My sisters and Jim were
in the room, as were Rachel Robinson, Jackie Robinson's
widow; my mother's nurse, Marie; and Mommy's obsequious lawyer. In the guest room, away from her bed, I burst
into a bout of keening. I was in another sphere, going deeper
and deeper into it, kneeling on the floor, dipping from one
side to another, wringing my hands, while Jim, Lucy, and
Joey did whatever they could to calm me down. It was spon-
taneous. It was otherworldly. It was fierce and completely
out of proportion. God only knows what it was—cellular,
placental, umbilical, or something else way, way beyond the
earth.

Oh, Mother. I didn't know that when you died I'd never
be me anymore.

As I was calling out her name, "Mother, Mother, Mother,"
the first line of the poem Jackie had been referencing came
back to me, the phrase lit up like a marquee in my brain.

Oh, Lord my God,
You called me from the sleep of nothingness
merely because of Your tremendous love.
You want to make good and beautiful beings.
You have called me by name in my mother's womb.
—JOSEPH TETLOW, SJ
  (FROM *HEARTS ON FIRE: PRAYING WITH JESUITS*)

The very next day, in one sitting, I wrote this song, "Like a River," for my mother.

Dear mother the struggle is over now
And your house is up for sale
We divided your railway watches
Between the four of us
I fought over the pearls
With the other girls
But it was all a metaphor
For what was wrong with us
As the room is emptying out
Your face so young comes into view
And on the back porch is a well-worn step
And a pool of light you can walk into

I'll wait no more for you like a daughter,
That part of our life together is over
But I will wait for you, forever
Like a river . . .

Can you clear up the mystery of the Sphinx?
Do you know any more about God?
Are you dancing with Benjamin Franklin
On the face of the moon?
Have you reconciled with Dad?
Does the rain still make you sad?
Last night I swear I could feel you
Moving through my room
And I thought you touched my feet
I so wanted it to be true
In my theater there is a stage
And a footlight you can step into . . .

I'll wait no more for you like a daughter,
That part of our life together is over
But I will wait for you, forever
Like a river . . .

In the river I know I will find the key
And your voice will rise like the spray
In the moment of knowing
The tide will wash away my doubt
'Cause you're already home
Making it nice for when I come home
Like the way I find my bed turned down
Coming in from a late night out.
Please keep reminding me
Of what in my soul I know is true

Come in my boat, there's a seat beside me
And two or three stars we can gaze into . . .

I'll wait no more for you like a daughter,
That part of our life together is over
But I will wait for you, forever
Like a river . . .

—"LIKE A RIVER"

And will I see you up in that heaven

In all its light will I know you're there

Will we say the things that we never dared

If wishing makes it so

Won't you let me know

That life is eternal

And love is immortal

And death is only a horizon

—"LIFE IS ETERNAL"

10

Only a Horizon

IN 2014, TWENTY YEARS AFTER JACKIE'S DEATH, I sat at my desk on the Vineyard and wrote her a long letter. She was always on my mind, and more so recently.

Dear Jackie:

It is in the future for some of us foolish souls not in the know. Perhaps you already know that Mike died, of a heart attack, a few weeks after his 84th birthday. I remember being the one who told Mike that you had died, and him crying over the phone. I heard him. It wasn't for pretense, or an arrangement of an action. No—Mike cried. He had said in an interview once, "I've always been impressed by the fact that upon entering a room full of people, you find them saying one thing, doing another, and wishing they were doing a third." I don't know for sure which of these represented his crying on the phone. It was surely a very sudden and unplanned response.

You were important enough to him, Jackie, that I found myself by association more important to both of you. For example, if so-and-so likes Lillian Hellman, then you seek her out to underline your value. It may be a schoolyard measure, but it works in romance; it works in Hollywood; it works in the workplace and of course in friendship.

One couldn't reach a higher position than you did. Some are only relevant for a short period of time when their movies or records are at the top of the charts. One-hit wonders, their popularity and panache and gain-by-association are limited; rats are seen visibly leaving the sinking ship and desperate measures are taken to revive the lifeless body. Though I'd only tell you this, I experienced this loss of power several times in my life and gained it back. It's hard to pin it down, but Mike, as you know, happened to be a measuring spoon of infinite precision. I could always tell where I stood in the

overall world's lineup based on his and my most recent
interchange. I saw myself through his eyes, which had
seen me through someone else's more suitably superior
eyes.

Mike and I continued to have the ups and downs
of a volatile, marriage-like relationship. One of two
self-loathing Jews who needed the other's mothering
nurturing—actually the nurturing of many mothers.
A few months before he died, he and Diane invited me
over to his house. The visit was warm, loving, a tying-up,
a P.S., an apology, an embrace. I'm so glad we had that
meeting.

I wish you were here with me right now, Jackie.
There's so much I've wanted to tell you. Not just things
from my own life, but the lives of other people we know.
Mike, of course, being first and foremost, since he was
the one who brought us together in so many ways both
mysterious and obvious. He was the tablecloth on which
you and I set down our table settings, and when that
tablecloth was whisked away at some point, I think you
and I were surprised and relieved and gratified that we
kept on eating and carrying on our conversation without
interruption, as if we'd never needed that tablecloth in
the first place or needed it only as a kind of insurance, as
a security blanket.

But now Mike is really gone, and of course the first
person I thought to tell was you, you whom I miss deeply

and think about every day, and will keep in the most
secure place in my heart for the rest of my own life.
My love to you always,
Carly

When Jackie died, I never thought I would come to think of her as belonging to the past. I would never say the words "I loved her" or "She used to . . ." or "Do you remember when she . . . ?" I would never use the past tense to describe her. As long as I was in the present, Jackie was, too. Which is why writing her a letter in the days after Mike died didn't feel remotely strange. It felt as natural as getting up in the morning or drinking tea.

It was as though Jackie was only a phone call or a windy walk through the springtime snow away. How is death different from any long separation from anyone you haven't seen, or spoken to on the phone, for a seeming eternity? The difference is that being alive, you can always bridge that separation by dialing their number or composing an email or letter—so how is that different from what I did on that frosty November day, just before Thanksgiving, when both Mike and Jackie were so very much on my mind?

I HAD COME TO REALIZE that when Jackie said that I had seen who she was, it was through the lens of my own painful relationships; I was plagued with running to men who I thought would save me. Certainly she inferred that Ari was the mistake she couldn't avoid, "like a collision of destructive mutual needs." I could see through her wise propaganda. Her way of keeping her cards close.

We weren't jealous of each other. We were proud. Nothing stoked envy of the other. Because we were of a different time period, we didn't go into a store and want the same thing. She was the wise older one who might have been relieved that I didn't want anything from her. Of course, I wanted her love, wanted to be a "we" and not a "them." There was nothing to be competitive over. We were in our own ball courts, each admiring and sharing in each other's serves and crying over each other's problems and sorrows. There turned out to be very little that was in the way. Our friendship was quite blessed in that sense. I hope to get to know her grandchildren, whom she completely adored and spent so much time with.

NOT LONG AFTER my mother died, Jackie and some of her best friends were gathered at my apartment at 135 Central Park West. They included Joe Armstrong, Peter Duchin, and his wife Brooke Hayward. At Jackie's suggestion, I also invited Ken Burns, who was finally making good on his rain-date promise. "I love Ken Burns!" Jackie told me on the phone. "I would love to meet him!"

That day, Ken dominated the conversation, answering all the many questions Jackie put to him. About baseball, too. Who knew that Jackie had a latent interest in baseball? Or was it merely the willing orator she had found in Ken, who shines through on any subject he's talking about? He wasted no time in congratulating her on the work she had done preserving Grand Central Terminal as a national monument. I remembered telling Jackie: "I've always wanted to do a concert there. Just be there, unannounced, as passengers walk through, getting off and on trains. I have such memories from my whole life, passing through en route to Riverdale, Stamford, Hudson." I asked her, "Why did you decide to focus your efforts on this particular building?"

"It was a romantic decision," she explained, "as so many of our decisions are. It's so life-affirming. Standing up for beauty, elegance, and history. I heard of its imminent demise on a day I was walking south and saw the Pan Am building rising above it, and I thought of what might happen if it mattered to no one." She turned to me. "Oh, Carly, *do* a concert there. It would be like putting an exclamation point on the city's decision to save this masterpiece."

I did a concert at Grand Central Terminal a year later, in that awesome carousel of trains. I was told the acoustics would be a nightmare and that the security would be hell. They weren't. It was a breeze. It stands alone as the most personal public performance I've ever given. Jackie died a year before that concert. And there it was again, hands reaching across time and space; our passions overlapping, the impossible made possible; the strength of the past indelibly imprinted on the present. I was so proud to sing in Grand Central Terminal. And I dedicated the concert to Jackie.

That day at my house, Jackie was fully present—more than I was—and though there were a few grim reminders of how sick she really was, they were, as always, unspoken, part of our continuous smile that made up the communal mask. Only when the two of us were alone for a minute did Jackie mention the wigs she would have to wear during the hot and humid summer ahead on the Vineyard.

Before Jackie left that afternoon, I gave her the lyrics to "Touched by the Sun," which I'd handwritten on a piece of paper. She called me as soon as she read it—which might have been in the car, on the way back to her apartment—and she seemed as excited by it as she had been about Ken's baseball stories. I told her that I'd written it about her, though I think she knew that already. Even if Jackie was in physical pain, she seemed tethered to the present, or at least the largest part of her was. She never let anyone see her wage war with fear. Her public commitment was to protocol. When she let her guard down with me, it was almost like the insertion of another person into the room.

Two weeks later, I was told that she'd made the decision to go home to her apartment and be with her family for her last days. The prognosis was terminal, and for her it was, as always, a private matter, just as her decision must have called on a strength that was inherent but also learned. I was at a loss to know what to say. I remember that pinnacle moment:

"I know you see through me." And I responded: "I want to be with you."

We spoke twice in that period between lunch at my house and the day of her death, our conversations warm. She veered away from telling me anything more about herself. Instead she wanted to know how I was dealing with my mother's death. From the stories I'd told her, and Mike's description of her, she'd intuited that my mother was formidable, and that my attachment to her was bedeviled.

Around the time of my mother's death, Jackie wrote me a letter on her powder-blue stationery. As she herself was so sick at the time, the energy it must have taken to sit down and write me was an act of love and pure selflessness. She said all the right things, all the things I needed to hear. That I had been a good daughter. That my mother must have been proud of me, even if she didn't always let me see that. That I had given enough of myself to her.

It was a letter I'd wanted to get in the mail from my own mother, but never had. One expressing a pure, tender pride in her daughter, unleavened by darker thoughts or impulses or rivalries. Of course, those blacker intervals will always be there in a family, but I also believe it is possible to express pride that doesn't circle back to oneself, or act from a position of permanently injured sacrifice. When I finished reading and rereading Jackie's letter, I was able to appreciate the height and width of the friendship and love that Jackie had given me for so many years. Not just her pride, her interest, her enthusiasm, but also her protection, the tender maternity she held out, and continued to hold out even through her own immense struggles.

Exactly one month after the party I'd held for her at my apartment, I called Jackie sometime in the late morning. Marta answered the phone. When I asked her how Jackie was doing, she said, "Madame is comfortable, but she is sedated." She would call me, she said, when she knew anything.

Immediately I called Joe Armstrong and told him. Jackie and Joe had a very real and close relationship. Joe was the only person I could think to call other than Mike, and I was having trouble reaching Mike. Joe, who lived eight blocks away, told me to meet him at his apartment, and I did. We were comforted by each other. Both of us believed in prayer, and in the idea that the bigger the number of people praying together in the same place at the same time, the greater the strength of that prayer.

Whenever I feel the need to intensify a prayer, I close my eyes and picture what it is I want in an extremely tense way. My eyebrows crinkle and wrinkle, and blood flushes my cheeks. It's not calm, it's hectic, adamant, because I want so badly for my prayer to be heard. As I prayed, I pictured Jackie in the summer that had yet to come, in her kayak, moving the paddle easily across calm water under a blue sky—a fair-weather rainbow symbolizing her return to health.

But I also remember that Joe and I both wore expressions

like the ones on children's faces as they're running in horror. It was almost impossible to "feel" the shock, the sadness, the missing, and the remembering showing up simultaneously. What's more, the world had begun to intrude with its collective mass awareness, and I had no idea what place my own private feelings about Jackie really had anymore. Were they more important, less important, the same? Did it matter?

The call from Marta came in the early afternoon. She was barely able to say the words. It wouldn't be long now, and if I wanted to say good-bye, now was the right time. She added, "She won't hear you."

Joe and I made our way across the park, from Eighty-first Street and Central Park West, going past the Delacorte Theater in the park, following paths I'd traversed more times than I could remember. We reached the East Side, and Jackie's building. A horrible amount of sun hovered and shone down on the pavement outside. It was as if the entire energy of the planet was focused on her, in a sharply defined gash of burning heat that should have been shadows and fog. There was now nothing to hide behind.

Dressed in jeans, my hair in a ponytail, I felt embarrassed to make my way forward like an intruder, in plain sight, through the crowds, past the barricades, my name on someone's list. In her silent presence, Jackie was still drawing people out. She would continue to exert as much control as the moment allowed. Whose rules were these? What book of etiquette was she following? I knew only that someone, something, some belief system, would carry the rest of us through, help us know what to do in place of what to feel—for certainly very few people knew how to feel. We all pretend our feelings matter.

Why at this moment was I searching for protocol, and not paying enough attention to my own emotions? *Do the right thing, Carly. Watch the others—watch Joe—and see what they do. Follow them, Carly.*

Joe and I took the elevator up to Jackie's apartment on the fifteenth floor, where we were told that only women were allowed to go inside her bedroom. Caroline and Ed were in the hallway. They were solemn, and understandably there was no attempt at greetings, or even nodding.

Just then I heard an uproar coming from the library adjacent to her bedroom, and wondered if Jackie could hear any of it. Irish voices raised in song? Drinking songs? I picked out Teddy's voice, then Pat Kennedy Lawford's, a slurred tumble of words ending in laughter. There were Shrivers there in the apartment, too, and Smiths, and the same line of demarcation present at Jackie's Labor Day parties—the raucous bearishness of the Hyannis Port contingent, mixed with friends of Jackie's, and the Bouviers, as well as other relatives whose expressions were more muted and, to my mind at least, better suited for the occasion.

Marta signaled for me to come into Madame's bedroom.

I walked gingerly past the library, the same one where

the book Jackie had made for Ari, too big for any bookcase, rested in a cabinet of rare brandies under her large antique desk. The library was where all the hoopla was coming from. All the drinking and Irish celebration made me anxious. Just maybe there was something wrong with it. Was the Kennedys' defiance of death part and parcel of a furious star that got crossed?

Jackie's bedroom was in one corner of the building and looked out over both Eighty-second Street and Fifth Avenue, the Metropolitan Museum only a toss away. The curtains were drawn, but enough light seeped through to illuminate everything and everyone. Fifteen floors below, on the sidewalks, the large and growing gathering was tame and respectful. The crowd might have been waving silently in slow motion, or at least I imagined they were. I wanted—I needed—poetry from them. Something South American. Something from García Márquez, like the couple in love on the ship's deck at the end of *Love in the Time of Cholera*. Sending everyone who had ever loved another person to seek out and find that person again. I entered Jackie's bedroom.

Bunny Mellon, a mahogany twist of a French braid at the back of her neck, was attired in fashionable black. She was sitting in a straight-backed upholstered chair on the side of the bed nearest the door. I closed the door as quietly as possible behind me. Her bed was canopied and feminine. Maurice stood at the end, with John beside him. I felt John's aloneness, and wished that Christina Haag, his girlfriend to whom I felt so close, was there to support him. Even though he was already with Daryl Hannah, I still believed he would return someday to Christina. She was like family.

At the same time, I didn't understand the ceremony of their presence—that is, if one was even being adhered to, or if the two of them were making it up as they went along. Both men, Jackie's close male companion and her son, looked impeccable in formal suits, light shirts, and somber ties. Their faces displayed hardly any emotion, or were they just difficult to read? Two sets of hands knotted at waist level as they watched over Jackie.

I nodded hello to them but didn't smile (which has always been hard for me, because I depend on my smile). Bunny was holding Jackie's right hand and her other hand clutched some prayer beads. She was saying soft words half under her breath. She noticed me. "You sit with her for a bit," she said kindly.

I did.

Closer to her now, I saw that Jackie's face was peaceful and relaxed, as if after a long climb up a mountain. Close up I could see that she was more magnificent now than I had ever seen her before. A beam of light landed on her bed from the open window, and as I picked up and held her hand, there was no hint that she was assisting me, yet it was weightless, which would imply that she herself was carrying some of that weight. Was there some part of her that was conscious? I couldn't tell. It was as though from our very different perspectives we were both looking at and seeing together the same singular and illuminated point in space.

What were the words going through her head now? I wondered. What could she be thinking? She, whose thoughts and chatter were mercurial and word-loving, their cadence eternally scattering. Was her brain forming words like "particular," breaking out through the octave, jumping up, ravishing the syllables with a hiccup of a vowel, streaming through like a singer carrying the final syllable with her breath? Words like "telegrams" and "visit from Ithaca" and "ubiquitous" and "needles"—but where is the thread? Did any pictures accompany or enhance those words? Could she see her late husband the president, or feel his presence? Her father's mother? Friends from early school days? Was she girding her wildest impulses even now? Was there a monotone to her prayers? Could she have sat up and asked everybody to go home?

Soon it would be violet light, that light within which the forgetting and the creation of a new concept of oneself merge. Would it be some uncertain station with a fine silk blanket? Perhaps one woven in the lower hemisphere of the planet? So deep blue it could almost assume the violet light that surrounded it. So smooth it could get confused in a chant from a lost century; swimming in unison between the strident fourths of the young boys' changing voices. Without modulation. Just the smoothness and beauty and absence of all time.

I loved this woman. *Loved* her. Jackie had, with me, always been so available, so accepting and present, and she had so much about her to love. And I had *felt* loved by her. My mind was a jumble. As I sat beside her bed, I had many reveries, but my words came out simply. I focused so hard, I wasn't aware that anyone else in the room could hear me. I loved her. And I told her that. Quietly.

Epilogue:
"Will It Soar Like Jazz on a Saxophone, or Evaporate on a Breeze?"

A FEW DAYS AFTER THAT LAST VISIT, Jim and I attended the wake at Jackie's apartment. I brought a copy of the lyrics to "Touched by the Sun," written out on a piece of parchment, which I handed to Bunny Mellon. I somehow knew she would be the best person to pass them along to. She would be a messenger to wherever they ended up living. She kissed me on the cheek and whispered, "I'll put it where you want it, Carly."

I get to imagine it at the will of the wind, high in the

skies over Paris, the hills of Spain and Africa, the rivers, the oceans, dipping now and then into that dark and loving night where there is no more chaos. Serene sun and grass waving, fertile fields, white clouds, up higher—close to the light.

I STARTED THESE PAGES by describing how hard it is to recapture a person you love. How despite all your efforts, in the end you're left with only bits and scraps of clay and color, partial versions of the real thing, half notes, not full ones, the effect that a funnel of the sun or moonlight has on a rug or an empty corner of a bedroom rather than the full sky itself. But maybe, as Jackie liked to tell me, I'm being too hard on myself.

Maybe those quarter tones and ounces and dashed-off moments and resting arms and fleeting gazes and traces of remembered laughter are what anybody is, and the person we try so hard to remember, and to complete, is just their holder, an estuary for those thousands of small things. So it is perhaps with Jackie, who resists capture and retains her privacy and mystery. But aren't we all participants in that very same mystery? I *do* know that some individuals are able to cast bigger, longer shadows than others, and what are shadows created by if not by light? Not light from a new or full moon, but light from a sun that selected Jackie early on as a favored native and let those in her small circle fill and replenish with reflected warmth, majesty, and kindness.

If she, Jackie, was touched by the sun—and she *was*— we, her friends who loved her, were touched by that sun, too.

If you want to be brave

And reach for the top of the sky

And the farthest point on the horizon

Do you know who you'll meet there

Great soldiers and seafarers

Artists and dreamers

Who need to be close, close to the light

They need to be in danger of burning by fire

And I, I want to get there

I, I want to be one

One who is touched by the sun

One who is touched by the sun

Often I want to walk

The safe side of the street

And lull myself to sleep

And dull my pain

But deep down inside I know

I've got to learn from the greats

Earn my right to be living

Let my wings of desire

Soar over the night

I need to let them say

"She must have been mad"

And I, I want to get there

I, I want to be one

One who is touched by the sun

One who is touched by the sun

I've got to learn from the greats

Earn my right to be living

With every breath that I take

Every heartbeat

I want to get there

I want to be one

One who is touched by the sun

One who is touched by the sun

—"TOUCHED BY THE SUN"

Acknowledgments

First, to my dear friend Jessica Hoffman Davis, whose floor I played dolls and jacks on, who I wrote my first song with, and stayed close friends with while she was writing books and holding a chair in education at Harvard and raising one of the largest families on the East Coast. Jesse stayed with this book from the first to the last page. In addition, I happen to love her.

To Peter Smith, my genuinely gracious and hugely engaging friend, whom I have grown to adore. He took the book in hand and helped to form it. He made sense out of my overgrown stacks of notes called things like "flat footed horse" and "Mr. Nose." I can only hope he will be a part of, an all-seer of, a tracker of, everything I endeavor to do.

To Colin Dickerman, my editor. You all know "company men," but you might not know that they are real people who not only pat you down but who encourage you and keep you in line and go to Morocco when your acknowledgments are due. They also, by the way, happen to edit your book. Don't let the dust blow in your eyes, advisor.

Also at FSG, thank you to Mitzi Angel, Janine Barlow, Thomas Colligan, Daniel del Valle, Nina Frieman, Jonathan Galassi, Ian Van Wye, and Sarita Varma.

Then to Bill Clegg: editor, friend, and agent. A formidable trio of responsibilities. Never has anyone been so crucial in the making, breaking, and supporting of a book. I was star-struck when I first met him because of the largeness of his literary persona. But he turned out to be just another passenger, and a terrific one, thank the Lord.

I am also very grateful for the love and support of Lucy, Joey, and Peter, my siblings, for simply being born and giving me their love and reflecting mirrors to help me see who I am. Also, to the family of Jackie Kennedy, who rounded out so much of what I was charmed to see in her. They chose me to be included in Caroline and Ed's wedding, which was really the start of our friendship.

To Richard, my captain, for reading through many drafts of the book and providing insight after insight, thus tightening up the book, originally 897 pages, down to something a little tidier. You don't know how much you mean to me.

To Sally and Ben, always.

And to the following people for just being around and supportive and helpful to the process of the often formidable task of writing a book, any book:

Al; Andreas; Arlyne; Billy Bob; Bodhi; Carinthia; Dana; Dean; Father Edward; Fernanda; Forte; Frank; Geoff; Harold; Jake, Misha and Zaya; Larry; Laurie; Matt and Andy; Meghan; Marc; Mia; Noah and Jules; Richard P.; Rose; Russell; Said and Ronald; Saw; Teese; Terrence; Trish.

A NOTE ABOUT THE AUTHOR

Carly Simon is a songwriter and singer of songs. Her children are Ben Taylor and Sally Taylor Bragonier. She has one grandchild: Bodhi Taylor Bragonier. She lives on Martha's Vineyard and is the author of *Boys in the Trees*.